THE STRUCTURE
OF
MAGIC
I

A Book about Language
and Therapy

By
RICHARD BANDLER
and
JOHN GRINDER

Science and Behavior Books, Inc.
Palo Alto, California 94306

Library of Congress Card Number 75-12452
ISBN 08314-0044-7

Cover design from an original oil painting expressly done for *Magic I* by Josh Doolan.

Typography by Penguin ≈ Santa Clara, California

DEDICATION

We dedicate this book
to
   Virginia Satir

in appreciation for giving us
   her intuitions about
      people.

These intuitions are
   the basis of what
      follows
         in this book.

Thank you, Virginia.
We
   love you.

TABLE OF CONTENTS

ACKNOWLEDGMENTS

We would like to thank all of those who have been helpful in the completion of this book: Jim Anderson and Kristofer Bakke, without whom this book would have taken twice as long, and the makers of Folgers Coffee, without whose fine product we would not have made it through the long nights.

FOREWORD

WOW! What could anyone say about having their work looked at by four fine eyes in the heads of two very capable human researchers? This book is the outcome of the efforts of two intriguing, smart, young men who are interested in finding out how change takes place and in documenting the process. They seem to have come up with a description of the predictable elements that make change happen in a transaction between two people. Knowing what these elements are makes it possible to use them consciously and, thus, to have useful methods for inducing change.

I often say to people that I have a right to be a slow learner but educable. What this means to me as a therapist is that I have only one thought — to help the people who come to me in pain to make changes in their lives. How I use my body, my voice, my eyes, my hands, in addition to the words and the way I use words, is my only tool. Since my goal is to make change possible for everyone, every someone offers a new challenge.

Looking back, I see that, although I was aware that change was happening, I was unaware of the specific elements that went into the transaction which made change possible. For years, I wondered what it would be like to be on the other end of me, to view myself working, to view the process of change from the other side. The authors spent hours looking at video tapes and listening to audio material, and they found patterns emerging which they could document. I do something, I feel it, I see it, my gut responds to it — that is a subjective experience. When I do it with someone else, their eyes, ears, body sense these things. What Richard Bandler and John Grinder have done is to watch the process of change over a time and to distill from it the patterns of the *how* process. What they learned relates particularly, in a sophisticated way, to mathematics, physics, neurology and linguistics.

It would be hard for me to write this Foreword without my own feeling of excitement, amazement and thrill coming through. I have been a teacher of family therapy for a long time, as well as a clinician and a theoretician. This means that I have seen change taking place in many families, and I have been involved in training many family therapists. I have a theory about *how* I make change occur. The knowledge of the process is now considerably advanced by Richard Bandler and John Grinder, who can talk in a way that can be concretized and measured about the ingredients of the *what* that goes into making the *how* possible.

Virginia M. Satir

INTRODUCTION

It is a strange pleasure to write an introduction for this book because John Grinder and Richard Bandler have done something similar to what my colleagues and I attempted fifteen years ago.

The task was easy to define: to create the beginnings of an appropriate theoretical base for the describing of human interaction.

The difficulty lay in the word "appropriate" and in the fact that what was to be described included not only the event sequences of successful communication but also the patterns of misunderstanding and the pathogenic.

The behavioral sciences, and especially psychiatry, have always avoided theory, and it is easy to make a list of the various maneuvers whereby theory could be avoided: the historians (and some anthropologists) chose the impossible task of making not *theory* but more *data* out of what was known — a task for detectives and courts of law. The sociologists trimmed the complex variations of known fact to such an ultimate simplicity that the clipped nuggets could be counted. Economists believed in transitive preference. Psychologists accepted all sorts of internal explanatory entities (ego, anxiety, aggression, instinct, conflict, etc.) in a way reminiscent of medieval psycho-theology.

Psychiatrists dabbled in all these methods of explanation; they searched for narratives of childhood to explain current behavior, making new data out of what was known. They attempted to create statistical samples of morbidity. They wallowed in internal and mythical entities, ids and archetypes. Above all, they borrowed the concepts of physics and mechanics — energy, tension, and the like — to create a scientism.

But there were a few beginnings from which to work: the "logical types" of Russell and Whitehead, the "Games Theory" of Von Neumann, the notions of comparable form (called "homology" by biologists), the concepts of "levels" in linguistics, Von Domarus' analysis of "schizophrenic" syllogisms, the notion of discontinuity in genetics and the related notion of binary information. Pattern and redundancy were beginning to be defined. And, above all, there was the idea of homeostasis and self-correction in cybernetics.

Out of these scattered pieces came a hierarchic classification of orders of message and (therefore) of orders of learning, the beginnings of a theory of "schizophrenia" and with it an attempt, very premature, to classify the ways in which people and animals code their messages (digital, analogic, iconic, kinesic, verbal, etc.).

Perhaps our greatest handicap at that time was the difficulty which the professionals seemed to experience when they tried to understand what we were doing. Some even tried to count "double binds" in recorded conversations. I treasure somewhere in my files a letter from a funding agency telling me that my work should be more clinical, more experimental, and, above all, more quantitative.

Grinder and Bandler have confronted the problems which we confronted then and this series is the result. They have tools which we did not have — or did not see how to use. They have succeeded in making linguistics into a base for theory and simultaneously into a tool for therapy. This gives them a double control over the psychiatric phenomena, and they have done something which, as I see it today, we were foolish to miss.

We already knew that most of the premises of individual psychology were useless, and we knew that we ought to classify modes of communicating. But it never occurred to us to ask about the effects of the modes upon interpersonal relations. In this first volume, Grinder and Bandler have succeeded in making explicit the syntax of how people avoid change and, therefore, how to assist them in changing. Here they focus on verbal communication. In the second volume, they develop a general model of communication and change involving the other modes of communication which human beings use to represent and communicate their experience. What happens when messages in digital mode are flung at an analog thinker? Or when visual presentations are offered to an auditory client?

We did not see that these various ways of coding — visual,

auditory, etc. — are so far apart, so mutually different even in neurophysiological representation, that no material in one mode can ever be of the same logical type as any material in any other mode.

This discovery seems obvious when the argument starts from linguistics, as in the first volume of the present series, instead of starting from culture contrast and psychosis, as we did.

But, indeed, much that was so difficult to say in 1955 is strikingly easier to say in 1975.

May it be heard!

> *Gregory Bateson*
> Kresge College
> University of California, Santa Cruz

Preface

Down through the ages the power and wonder of practitioners of magic have been recorded in song and story. The presence of wizards, witches, sorcerers, shamen, and gurus has always been intriguing and awe inspiring to the average person. These people of power, wrapped in a cloak of secrecy, presented a striking contradiction to the common ways of dealing with the world. The spells and incantations they wove were feared beyond belief and, at the same time, sought constantly for the help they could provide. Whenever these people of power publicly performed their wonders, they would both shatter the concepts of reality of that time and place and present themselves as having something that was beyond learning. In modern time, the mantle of the wizard is most often placed upon those dynamic practitioners of psychotherapy who exceed the skill of other therapists by leaps and bounds, and whose work is so amazing to watch that it moves us with powerful emotions, disbelief, and utter confusion. Just as with all wizards of the ages of the earth whose knowledge was treasured and passed down from sage to sage — losing and adding pieces but retaining a basic structure — so, too, does the magic of these therapeutic wizards also have structure.

The Prince and the Magician

Once upon a time there was a young prince who believed in all things but three. He did not believe in princesses, he did not believe in islands, he did not believe in God. His father, the king, told him that such things did not exist. As there were no princesses or islands in his father's domains, and no sign of God, the prince believed his father.

But then, one day, the prince ran away from his palace and came to the next land. There, to his astonishment, from every coast he saw islands, and on these islands, strange and troubling creatures whom he dared not name. As he was searching for a boat, a man in full evening dress approached him along the shore.

"Are those real islands?" asked the young prince.

"Of course they are real islands," said the man in evening dress.

"And those strange and troubling creatures?"

"They are all genuine and authentic princesses."

"Then God must also exist!" cried the prince.

"I am God," replied the man in evening dress, with a bow.

The young prince returned home as quickly as he could.

"So, you are back," said his father, the king.

"I have seen islands, I have seen princesses, I have seen God," said the prince reproachfully.

The king was unmoved.

"Neither real islands, nor real princesses, nor a real God exist."

"I saw them!"

"Tell me how God was dressed."

"God was in full evening dress."

"Were the sleeves of his coat rolled back?"

The prince remembered that they had been. The king smiled.

"That is the uniform of a magician. You have been deceived."

At this, the prince returned to the next land and went to the same shore, where once again he came upon the man in full evening dress.

"My father, the king, has told me who you are," said the prince indignantly. "You deceived me last time, but not again. Now I know that those are not real islands and real princesses, because you are a magician."

The man on the shore smiled.

"It is you who are deceived, my boy. In your father's kingdom, there are many islands and many princesses. But you are under your father's spell, so you cannot see them."

The prince pensively returned home. When he saw his father, he looked him in the eye.

"Father, is it true that you are not a real king, but only a magician?"

The king smiled and rolled back his sleeves.

"Yes, my son, I'm only a magician."

"Then the man on the other shore was God."

"The man on the other shore was another magician."

"I must know the truth, the truth beyond magic."

"There is no truth beyond magic," said the king.

The prince was full of sadness. He said, "I will kill myself."

The king by magic caused death to appear. Death stood in the door and beckoned to the prince. The prince shuddered. He remembered the beautiful but unreal islands and the unreal but beautiful princesses.

"Very well," he said, "I can bear it."

"You see, my son," said the king, "you, too, now begin to be a magician."

Reprinted from *The Magus*, by John Fowles,
Dell Publishing Co., Inc.; pp. 499-500.

Warning to the Reader

The central task of psychology, whether experimental or applied, is the understanding of human behavior. Human behavior is extremely complex. To say, however, that our behavior is complex is not to deny that it has structure. In general, modern psychology has attempted to understand human behavior by breaking it down into relatively separate areas of study — for example, the areas of perception, of learning, of language behavior, of motor skills. As our understanding of each of these areas grows, we continue to uncover the structure of the human behavior being described — to find that human behavior is rule governed.

To say that human behavior is rule governed is not to say that we can understand it in simple stimulus-response terms. In the study of human languages, for example, the kind of rules required to describe this behavior is beyond the capabilities of S-R theories (Chomsky, 1957). It is useful for an adequate understanding of this book that you distinguish between rule-governed behavior and determined behavior.

Continuing with the example of human languages, the number of possible sentences in each human language (e.g., English, Spanish, etc.) is infinite. In other words, the number of verbal descriptions of human experiences is limitless. At the same time, the number of forms (syntax) in which this infinite set of meanings is represented is highly restricted — has structure — and, therefore, may be described by a set of rules. This sequence of words is an English sentence. It has structure, as can be demon-

strated by considering the result of reversing the order of words:
Sentence English an is words of sequence this.

Similarly, in the case of other types of complex human behavior, there is an infinite number of distinct acts. The form of these acts will have structure — and, therefore, will be describable by some set of rules. To say that human behavior is describable by some set of rules is not to warrant that our behavior is determined or predictable.

The most sophisticated study of human, rule-governed behavior is the study of human language systems. Specifically, a group of linguists known as transformational grammarians has developed a set of rules describing the forms which we use to represent and communicate our experience with language. Although transformational grammar is a young discipline (initiated in 1955), it has already had a profound effect on experimental psychology, especially modern learning theory. It has yet to have an impact on applied psychology. This book is designed to make the insights of transformational grammar available and usable to those people who work with complex human behavior.

There are three important pieces of information in addition to the above background which we want you to have as you begin this book:

1. What's in the book;
2. How to use the book;
3. What you can expect to gain from using the book.

1. What's in the Book

This book is designed to give you an explicit set of tools which will help you to become a more effective therapist. Chapter 1 shows that we do not operate directly on the world in which we live, but rather that we create models or maps of the world and use these maps to guide our behavior. Further, it states that effective therapy implies some change in the way that a client represents his experience.

Chapter 2 shows you the structure of one specific way human beings represent their experiences — human language systems. Chapter 3 presents a way of using the structure of language systems as a set of tools for operating in therapy. These tools are compatible with every form of psychotherapy of which we are aware. Chapter 4 presents a step-by-step procedure for learning and using these tools. Chapter 5 is composed of two transcripts with commentary showing the use of these tools in therapy. Chapter 6 integrates these tools with a number of well-known, non-verbal techniques from already established forms of psychotherapy.

2. How to Use this Book

This book is not a novel, and we recommend that you not attempt to read it as you would a novel. This book is a manual to teach you a set of tools which will increase your effectiveness as a therapist. As with any manual, it should be read and reread.

To begin this learning process for yourself, a general overall understanding of Chapters 1, 2, and 3 is adequate. Naturally, the more thoroughly you understand these chapters, the more effectively you will be able to apply the specific techniques presented in Chapter 4.

When you reach Chapter 4, slow down. This chapter consists of a set of step-by-step instructions to give you practice in the use of the techniques. Since this book, the first of a series, is primarily concerned with verbal techniques, most of the techniques are questions based on the *form* of the client's communication in therapy. Each of the techniques presented in Chapter 4 should be studied by itself in order to give you the optimum skill to increase your effectiveness as a therapist. Each of these techniques has at least one step-by-step exercise. To acquire these skills, you must practice them — USE THE EXERCISES.

Chapter 5 is *not* an example of what we regard as powerful therapy. Chapter 5 is designed to show you how the various techniques work in conjunction with one another. Read through the transcript with its commentary, paying attention to the choices that the therapist has and the flow of the verbal exchange between the therapist and the client. You may also wish to cover the commentary and to consider each of the client's sentences in turn, to determine whether you can identify all of the choices each of these sentences presents to you as a therapist.

Read through Chapter 6 carefully — its purpose is to teach you to use Chapter 4 techniques to identify the appropriateness of some of the better known, non-verbal techniques. If any of the non-verbal techniques presented in this chapter are techniques in which you are already trained, use them as a reference point to integrate other techniques which you find useful in your therapy. If none of your specific techniques is presented, pay particular attention to which of the Chapter 4 techniques you are using in therapy when you become aware of an appropriate place for you to employ one of your own specific techniques. This will begin the process of integration of the tools presented in this manual with your own style of therapy.

3. What You Can Expect to Gain from Using this Book

Using this book in the way we suggest will make you a more

effective therapist. This will happen specifically by:

1. Learning a specific set of questioning techniques based on the client's verbal communications;
2. Learning how the use of particular non-verbal techniques may be indicated by verbal cues.

The overall effect of this knowledge will be to give you a clear, explicit strategy for your work in therapy.

Chapter 1

THE STRUCTURE OF CHOICE

> ... operations of an almost mysterious character, which
> run counter to ordinary procedure in a more or less para-
> doxical way. They are methods which give an onlooker the
> impression of magic if he be not himself initiated or
> equally skilled in the mechanism.
>
> H. Vaihinger, *The Philosophy of As If*, p. 11

Out of the ranks of modern psychotherapy have emerged a number of charismatic superstars. These people seemingly perform the task of clinical psychology with the ease and wonder of a therapeutic magician. They reach into suffering, pain, and deadness of others, transforming their hopelessness into joy, life and renewed hope. Though the approaches they bring to this task seem varied and as different as day and night, they all seem to share a unique wonder and potency. Sheldon Kopp described his experience of one such person in his book *Guru* (p. 146):

> Perls had enormously powerful personal presence, inde-
> pendence of spirit, willingness to risk going wherever his
> intuitive feelings took him, and a profound capacity to be
> intimately in touch with anyone who was open to working
> with him. . . . It is not unusual to find yourself in tears, or
> exhausted, or joyful, after watching another being guided
> through such an experience. So brilliant was his intuition
> and so powerful were his techniques that sometimes it
> took Perls only minutes to reach the person on the hot
> seat. You might be some stuck, rigid, long-dead character,

seeking help and yet fearing that it would come and change things. He would put you on the hot seat, then do his magic. If you were willing to work, it was almost as though he could reach over, take hold of the zipper on your facade, and pull it down so quickly that your tortured soul would fall out onto the floor between the two of you.

Perls was not, and most certainly is not, the only therapist to present himself or herself with such magical potency. Virginia Satir and others we know seem to have this magical quality. To deny this capacity or to simply label it *talent, intuition,* or *genius* is to limit one's own potential as a people-helper. By doing this, one misses the opportunity to learn to offer those people who come to us an experience which they may use to change their lives to enjoy the fullness of living. Our desire in this book is not to question the magical quality of our experience of these therapeutic wizards, but rather to show that this magic which they perform — like other complex human activities such as painting, composing music, or placing a man on the moon — has structure and is, therefore, learnable, given the appropriate resources. Neither is it our intention to claim that reading a book can insure that you will have these dynamic qualities. We especially do not wish to make the claim that we have discovered the "right" or most powerful approach to psychotherapy.[1] We desire only to present you with a specific set of tools that seem to us to be implicit in the actions of these therapists, so that you may begin or continue the never-ending process to improve, enrich, and enlarge the skills you offer as a people-helper.

Since this set of tools is not based upon some pre-existing psychological theory or therapeutic approach, we would like to present the simple overview of the human processes out of which we have created these tools. We call this process *modeling.*

Through a Glass Darkly

Where the logical function actively intervenes, it alters what is given and causes it to depart from reality. We cannot even describe the elementary processes of the psyche without at every step meeting this disturbing — or shall we say helpful? — factor. As soon as sensation has entered the sphere of the psyche, it is drawn into the whirlpool of the logical processes. The psyche quite of its own accord alters both what is given and presented. Two things are to be distinguished in this process: First, the actual forms in which this change takes place; and secondly, the products obtained from the original material by this change.

The organized activity of the logical function draws into itself all the sensations and constructs an inner world of its own, which progressively departs from reality but yet at certain points still retains so intimate a connection with it that transitions from one to the other continually take place and we hardly notice that we are acting on a double stage — our own inner world (which, of course, we objectify as the world of sense-perception) and also an entirely different and external world.

H. Vaihinger, *The Philosophy of As If*, pp. 159-160

A number of people in the history of civilization have made this point — that there is an irreducible difference between the world and our experience of it. We as human beings do not operate directly on the world. Each of us creates a representation of the world in which we live — that is, we create a map or model which we use to generate our behavior. Our representation of the world determines to a large degree what our experience of the world will be, how we will perceive the world, what choices we will see available to us as we live in the world.

It must be remembered that the object of the world of ideas as a whole [the map or model — RWB/JTG] is not the portrayal of reality — this would be an utterly impossible task — but rather to provide us with an instrument for finding our way about more easily in the world.

H. Vaihinger, *The Philosophy of As If*, p. 15.

No two human beings have exactly the same experiences. The model that we create to guide us in the world is based in part upon our experiences. Each of us may, then, create a different model of the world we share and thus come to live in a somewhat different reality.

. . . important characteristics of maps should be noted. A map is not the territory it represents, but, if correct, it has a similar structure to the territory, which accounts for its usefulness. . .

A. Korzybski, *Science & Sanity*, 4th Ed., 1958, pp. 58-60.

We want to make two points here. First, there is a necessary difference between the world and any particular model or representation of the world. Second, the models of the world that each of us creates will themselves be different. There are a number of ways in which this can be demonstrated. For our purposes, we have divided them into three areas:[2] neurological constraints, social constraints, and individual constraints.

EXPERIENCE AND PERCEPTION AS AN ACTIVE PROCESS

Neurological Constraints

Consider the human receptor systems: sight, hearing, touch, taste, and smell. There are physical phenomena which lie outside the limits of these five accepted sensory channels. For example, sound waves either below 20 cycles per second or above 20,000 cycles per second cannot be detected by human beings. Yet these physical phenomena are structurally the same as the physical waves which fall between these limiting figures: the physical waves which we call *sound*. In the human visual system, we are able to detect wave forms only between 380 and 680 milli-microns. Wave forms above or below these figures are not detectable by the human eye. Again, we perceive only a portion of a continuous physical phenomenon as determined by our genetically given neurological limitations.

The human body is sensitive to touch — to contact on the surface of the skin. The sense of touch provides an excellent example of the profound influence our own neurological system can have on our experience. In a series of experiments (Boring, 1957, pp. 110-111) over a century ago, Weber established the fact that precisely the same real world situation is perceived by a human being as two totally distinct tactile experiences. In his experiments, Weber found that our ability to perceive being touched at two points on the surface of our skin varied dramatically depending upon where on the human body the two points were located. The smallest distance between two points which are experienced as two separate points on the little finger must be expanded thirty times before the two points can be distinguished when applied to the upper arm. Thus, a whole range of identical, real-world stimulus situations are perceived as two totally different experiences solely as a function of our nervous system. When touched on the little finger, we experience it as being touched in two places, and on the upper arm as being touched in one place. The physical world remains constant and our experience of it shifts dramatically as a function of our nervous system.

Similar differences between the world and our experience of it can be demonstrated for the other senses (Boring, 1957). The limitations of our perception are clearly recognized by scientists conducting experiments with the physical world as they develop machines which extend these limits. These instruments sense phenomena which lie outside the range of our senses, or outside of our ability to discriminate, and present them as signals which fall within our sensory range — signals such as photographs, pressure gauges, thermometers, oscilloscopes, Geiger counters, and alpha wave detectors. Thus, one way in which our models of the world will necessarily differ from the world itself is that our nervous system systematically distorts and deletes whole portions of the real world. This has the effect of reducing the range of possible human experience as well as introducing differences between what is actually going on in the world and our experience of it. Our nervous system, then, initially determined genetically, constitutes the first set of filters which distinguish the world — the territory — from our representations of the world — the map.

THROUGH A GLASS DARKLY WITH GLASSES WITH SOCIAL PRESCRIPTIONS

Social Constraints

... The suggestion is that the function of the brain and nervous system and sense organs is in the main eliminative and not productive. Each person is at each moment capable of remembering all that has ever happened to him and of perceiving everything that is happening everywhere in the universe. The function of the brain and the nervous system is to protect us from being overwhelmed and confused by this mass of largely useless and irrelevant knowledge, by shutting out most of what we should otherwise perceive or remember at any moment, and leaving only that very small and special selection which is likely to be practically useful. According to such a theory, each one of us is potentially Mind at Large. ... To make biological survival possible, Mind at Large has to be funneled through the reducing valve of the brain and nervous system. What comes out the other end is a measly trickle of the kind of consciousness which will help us to stay alive on the surface of this particular planet. To formulate and express the contents of this reduced awareness, man has invented and endlessly elaborated upon those symbol-systems and implicit philosophies which we call languages. Every individual is at once the beneficiary and the victim of the linguistic tradition into which he has been born — the beneficiary inasmuch as language gives access to the accumulated record of other people's experience, the victim insofar as it confirms in him the belief that reduced awareness is the only awareness, and as it bedevils his sense of reality, so that he is all too apt to take his concepts for data, his words for actual things.

Aldous Huxley, *The Doors of Perception*, New York: Harper & Row, 1954, pp. 22-23.

A second way in which our experience of the world differs from the world itself is through the set of social constraints or filters (prescription glasses) — we refer to these as social genetic factors.[3] By social genetics, we refer to all the categories or filters to which we are subject as members of a social system: our language, our accepted ways of perceiving, and all the socially agreed upon fictions.

Perhaps the most commonly recognized social genetic filter is our language system. Within any particular language system, for example, part of the richness of our experience is associated with the number of distinctions made in some area of our sensation.[4] In Maidu, an American Indian language of Northern California, only three words[5] are available to describe the color spectrum. They divide the spectrum as follows (the English words given are the closest approximations):

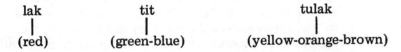

lak	tit	tulak
(red)	(green-blue)	(yellow-orange-brown)

While human beings are capable of making 7,500,000 different color distinctions in the visible color spectrum (Boring, 1957), the people who are native speakers of Maidu habitually group their experience into the three categories supplied by their language. These three Maidu color terms cover the same range of real-world sensation which the eight (specific) color terms of English do. Here the point is that a person who speaks Maidu is characteristically conscious of only three categories of color experience while the English speaker has more categories and, therefore, more habitual perceptual distinctions. This means that, while English speakers will describe their experience of two objects as different (say, a yellow book and an orange book), speakers of Maidu will typically describe their experience of the identical real-world situation as being the same (two *tulak* books).

Unlike our neurological genetic limitations, those introduced by the social genetic filters are easily overcome. This is most clearly demonstrated by the fact that we are able to speak more than one language — that is, we are able to use more than one set of social linguistic categories or filters to organize our experience, to serve as our representation of the world.[6] For example, take the ordinary sentence: *The book is blue. Blue* is the name that we, as native speakers of English, have learned to use to describe our experience of a certain portion of the continuum of visible light. Misled by the structure of our language, we come to assume that *blue* is a property of the object that we refer to as book rather than being the name which we have given our sensation.

In perception, the sensation complex *sweet-white* is constantly occurring in the substance *sugar*. The psyche then applies to this combination the category of a thing and its attributes: *The sugar is sweet*. Here, however, the *white* appears also as an object. *Sweet* is an attribute. The psyche is acquainted with the sensation *white* in other cases, where it appears as an attribute, so that, in this case too, white is treated as an attribute. But the category thing-attribute is inapplicable if *sweet* and *white* are attributes and no other sensation is given. Here language comes to our help, and by applying the name *sugar* to the whole perception, enables us to treat the single sensation as attributes. . . . Who authorized thought to assume that *white* was a thing, that *sweet* was an attribute? What right had it to go on to assume that both were attributes and then mentally add an object as their carrier? The justification can be found neither in the sensations themselves nor in what we now regard as reality. . . . All that is given to consciousness is sensation. By adding a Thing to which sensations are supposed to adhere as attributes, thought commits a very serious error. It hypostasizes sensation, which in the last analysis is only a process, as a subsistent attribute, and ascribes this *attribute* to a *thing* that either exists only in the complex of sensations itself, or has been simply added by thought to what has been sensed. . . . Where is the *sweet* that is ascribed to the sugar? It exists only in the act of sensation. . . . Thought not only changes immediate sensation thereby, but withdraws further and further from reality and becomes increasingly entangled in its own forms. By means of the *creative faculty* — to use this scientific term — it has invented a Thing which is supposed to possess an Attribute. This Thing is a fiction, the Attribute as such is a fiction, and the whole relationship is a fiction.

H. Vaihinger, *The Philosophy of As If*, p. 167.

The categories of experience which we share with other members of the social situation in which we live — for example, the common languge which we share — are a second way in which our models of the world differ from the world itself.

Notice that, in the case of the neurological constraints, in normal circumstances, the neurological filters are the same for all human beings — this is the common basis of experience that we share as members of the species. The social genetic filters are the same for the members of the same social-linguistic community but there are a large number of different social-linguistic communities. Thus, the second set of filters begins to distinguish us from each other as human beings. Our experiences begin to differ more radically, giving rise to more dramatically different representations of the world. The third set of constraints — the individual constraints — are the basis for the most far-reaching differences among us as humans.

THROUGH A GLASS DARKLY WITH GLASSES WITH INDIVIDUAL PRESCRIPTIONS

Individual Constraints

A third way in which our experience of the world can differ from the world itself is through a set of filters we call individual constraints. By individual constraints we refer to all the representations we create as human beings based upon our unique personal history. Every human being has a set of experiences which constitute his own personal history and are as unique to him as are his fingerprints. Just as every person has a set of distinct fingerprints, so, too, does each person have novel experiences of growing up and living, and no two life histories will ever be identical. Again, though they may have similarities, at least some aspects are different and unique to each person. The models or maps that we create in the process of living are based upon our individual experiences, and, since some aspects of our experiences will be unique to us as a person, some parts of our model of the world will be singular to each of us. These uncommon ways each of us represents the world will constitute a set of interests, habits, likes, dislikes, and rules for behavior which are distinctly our own. These differences in our experiences will guarantee that each of us has a model of the world which in some way will be different from any other person's model of the world.

For example, two identical twins might grow up together in the same home with the same parents, having almost identical experiences, but each, in the process of watching their parents relate to each other and to the rest of the family, might model their experiences differently. One might say: my parents never loved each other very much — they always argued, and my twin sister was the favorite — while the other might say: my parents really cared about each other — they discussed everything extensively and they really favored my twin sister. Thus, even in the limiting case of identical twins, their experiences as persons will give rise to differences in the way they create their own models or perceptions of the world. In cases in which our discussion is of unrelated persons, the differences created in personal models will be greater and more pervasive.

This third set of filters, the individual constraints, constitutes the basis for the profound differences among us as humans and the way we create models of the world. These differences in our models can either be ones that alter our prescriptions (socially given) in a way that enriches our experience and offers us more choices, or ones that impoverish our experience in a way that limits our ability to act effectively.

MODELS AND THERAPY

Our experience has been that, when people come to us in therapy, they typically come with pain, feeling themselves paralyzed, experiencing no choices or freedom of action in their lives. What we have found is not that the world is too limited or that there are no choices, but that these people block themselves from seeing those options and possibilities that are open to them since they are not available in their models of their world.

Almost every human being in our culture in his life cycle has a number of periods of change and transition which he must negotiate. Different forms of psychotherapy have developed various categories for these important transition-crisis points. What's peculiar is that some people are able to negotiate these periods of change with little difficulty, experiencing these periods as times of intense energy and creativity. Other people, faced with the same challenges, experience these periods as times of dread and pain — periods to be endured, when their primary concern is simple survival. The difference between these two groups appears to us to be primarily that the people who respond creatively to and cope effectively with this stress are people who have a rich representation or model of their situation, one in which they perceive a wide range of options in choosing their actions. The other people experience themselves as having few options, none of which are attractive to them — the "natural loser" game. The question for us is: How is it possible for different human beings faced with the same world to have such different experiences? Our understanding is that this difference follows primarily from differences in the richness of their models. Thus, the question becomes: How is it possible for human beings to maintain an impoverished model which causes them pain in the face of a multi-valued, rich, and complex world?

In coming to understand how it is that some people continue to cause themselves pain and anguish, it has been important for us to realize that they are not bad, crazy, or sick. They are, in fact, making the best choices from those of which they are aware, that is, the best choices available in their own particular model. In other words, human beings' behavior, no matter how bizarre it may first appear to be, makes sense when it is seen in the context of the choices generated by their model.[7] The difficulty is not that they are making the wrong choice, but that they do not have enough choices — they don't have a richly focused image of the world. The most pervasive paradox of the human condition which we see is that the processes which allow us to survive, grow, change, and experience joy are the same processes which allow us to maintain an impoverished model of the world — our ability to manipulate symbols, that is, to create models. So the processes which allow us to accomplish the most extraordinary and unique human activities are the same processes which block our further growth if we commit the error of mistaking the model for the reality. We can identify three general mechanisms by which we do this:[8] Generalization, Deletion, and Distortion.

Generalization is the process by which elements or pieces of a person's model become detached from their original experience and come to represent the entire category of which the experience is an example. Our ability to generalize is essential to coping with the world. For example, it is useful for us to be able to generalize from the experience of being burned when we touch a hot stove to a rule that hot stoves are not to be touched. But to generalize this experience to a perception that stoves are dangerous and, therefore, to refuse to be in the same room with one is to limit unnecessarily our movement in the world.

Suppose that the first few times a child is around a rocking chair, he leans on the back and falls over. He might come to a rule for himself that rocking chairs are unstable and refuse to ever try them again. If this child's model of the world lumps rocking chairs with chairs in general, then all chairs fall under the rule: Don't lean on the back! Another child who creates a model which distinguishes rocking chairs from other kinds of chairs has more choices in her behavior. From her experience, she develops a new rule or generalization for using rocking chairs only — Don't lean on the back! — and, therefore, has a richer model and more choices.

The same process of generalization may lead a human being to establish a rule such as "Don't express feelings." This rule in the context of a prisoner-of-war camp may have a high survival value and will allow the person to avoid placing himself in a position of being punished. However, that person, using this same rule in a marriage, limits his potential for intimacy by excluding expressions which are useful in that relationship. This may lead him to have feelings of loneliness and disconnectedness — here the person feels that he has no choice, since the possibility of expressing feelings is not available within his model.

The point here is that the same rule will be useful or not, depending upon the context — that is, that there are no right generalizations, that each model must be evaluated in its context. Furthermore, this gives us a key to understanding human behavior that seems to us to be bizarre or inappropriate — that is, if we can see the person's behavior in the context in which it originated.

A second mechanism which we can use either to cope effectively or to defeat ourselves is *Deletion.* Deletion is a process by which we selectively pay attention to certain dimensions of our experience and exclude others. Take, for example, the ability that people have to filter out or exclude all other sound in a room full of people talking in order to listen to one particular person's voice. Using the same process, people are able to block themselves from hearing messages of caring from other people who are important to them. For example, a man who was convinced that he was not worth caring about complained to us that his wife never gave him messages of caring. When we visited this man's home, we became aware that the man's wife did, indeed, express messages of caring to him. However, as these messages conflicted with the generalization that the man had made about his own self-worth, he literally did not hear his wife. This was verified when we called the man's attention to some of these messages, and the man stated that he had not even heard his wife when she had said those things.

Deletion reduces the world to proportions which we feel capable of handling. The reduction may be useful in some contexts and yet be the source of pain for us in others.

The third modeling process is that of *Distortion*. Distortion is the process which allows us to make shifts in our experience of sensory data. Fantasy, for example, allows us to prepare for experiences which we may have before they occur. People will distort present reality when rehearsing a speech which they will later present. It is this process which has made possible all the artistic creations which we as humans have produced. A sky as represented in a painting by Van Gogh is possible only as Van Gogh was able to distort his perception of the time-place in which he was located at the moment of creation. Similarly, all the great novels, all the revolutionary discoveries of the sciences involve the ability to distort and misrepresent present reality. Using the same technique, people can limit the richness of their experience. For example, when our friend mentioned earlier (who had made the generalization that he was not worth caring for) had the caring messages from his wife pointed out to him, he immediately distorted them. Specifically, each time that he heard a caring message that he had previously been deleting, he turned to us, smiling, and said, "She just says that because she wants something." In this way, the man was able to avoid allowing his experience to contradict the model of the world he had created, and, thereby, he prevented himself from having a richer representation, blocking himself from a more intimate and satisfying relationship with his wife.

A person who has at some time in his life been rejected makes the generalization that he's not worth caring for. As his model has this generalization, he either deletes caring messages or he reinterprets these messages as insincere. As he is unaware of any caring messages from others, he is able to maintain the generalization that he isn't worth caring about. This description is an example of the classical positive feedback loop: the self-fulfilling prophecy, or forward feedback (Pribram, 1967). A person's generalizations or expectations filter out and distort his experience to make it consistent with those expectations. As he has no experiences which challenge his generalizations, his expectations are confirmed and the cycle continues. In this way people maintain their impoverished models of the world.

Consider the classical psychological set or expectancy experiment by Postman and Bruner:

> ... In a psychological experiment that deserves to be far better known outside the trade, Bruner and Postman asked

experimental subjects to identify on short and controlled exposure a series of playing cards. Many of the cards were normal, but some were made anomalous, e.g., a red six of spades and a black four of hearts. Each experimental run was constituted by the display of a single card to a single subject in a series of gradually increased exposures. After each exposure the subject was asked what he had seen, and the run was terminated by two successive correct identifications.

Even on the shortest exposures many subjects identified most of the cards, and after a small increase all the subjects identified them all. For the normal cards these identifications were usually correct, but the anomalous cards were almost always identifed, without apparent hesitation or puzzlement, as normal. The black four of hearts might, for example, be identified as the four of either spades or hearts. Without any awareness of trouble, it was immediately fitted to one of the conceptual categories prepared by prior experience. One would not even like to say that the subjects had seen something different from what they identified. With a further increase of exposure to the anomalous cards, subjects did begin to hesitate and to display awareness of anomaly. Exposed, for example, to the red six of spades, some would say: That's the six of spades, but there's something wrong with it — the black has a red border. Further increase of exposure resulted in still more hesitation and confusion until finally, and sometimes quite suddenly, most subjects would produce the correct identification without hesitation. Moreover, after doing this with two or three of the anomalous cards, they would have little further difficulty with the others. A few subjects, however, were never able to make the requisite adjustment of their categories. Even at forty times the average exposure required to recognize normal cards for what they were, more than 10 per cent of the anomalous cards were not correctly identified. And the subjects who then failed often experienced acute personal distress. One of them exclaimed: "I can't make the suit out, whatever it is. It didn't even look like a card that time. I don't know what color it is now or whether it's a spade or a heart. I'm not even sure now what a spade looks like. My God!" In the next section we shall occasionally see scientists behaving this way, too.

Either as a metaphor or because it reflects the nature

of the mind, that psychological experiment provides wonderfully simple and cogent schema for the process of scientific discovery. In science, as in the playing card experiment, novelty emerges only with difficulty, manifested by resistance, against a background provided by expectation. Initially, only the anticipated and usual are experienced even under circumstances where anomaly is later to be observed.

The generalization that the people in the experiment made was that the possible color/shape pair would be the same as they had always experienced: black with clubs and spades, red with hearts and diamonds. They supported their generalization by distorting either the shape or color dimensions in the anomalous cards. The point is that, even in this simple task, the mechanism of generalization and its supporting process of distortion prevented the people from correctly identifying what was possible for them to see. The identification of funny-looking cards flashed onto a screen does little for us. However, the experiment is useful in that it's simple enough to show the same mechanisms which give us the potential of enriching or impoverishing all that happens to us as human beings — whether we are driving a car, attempting and achieving intimacy in a relationship, or, literally, what we will experience in every dimension of our lives.

SO WHAT?

The therapeutic "wizards" we described earlier come from various approaches to psychotherapy and use techniques that appear to be dramatically different. They describe the wonders they perform with terminologies so distinctive that their perceptions of what they do seem to have nothing in common. Many times we have watched these people working with someone and heard comments from onlookers which implied that these wizards of therapy make fantastic intuitive leaps which make their work incomprehensible. Yet, while the techniques of these wizards are different, they share one thing: They introduce changes in their clients' models which allow their clients more options in their behavior. What we see is that each of these wizards has a map or model for changing their clients' models of the world — i.e., a Meta-model — which allows them to effectively expand and enrich their clients' models in some way that makes the clients' lives richer and more worth living.

Our purpose in this book is to present to you an explicit Meta-model, that is, a Meta-model which is learnable. We want to make this Meta-model available to anyone who wishes to expand and enrich the skills they have as people-helpers. Since one of the main ways in which therapists can come to know and understand their clients is through language, and since language is also one of the primary ways all humans model their experiences, we have focused our work on the language of therapy. Fortunately, an explicit model of the structure of language has been developed independent of the context of psychology and therapy by transformational grammarians. Adapted for use in therapy, it offers us an explicit Meta-model for the enrichment and expansion of our therapeutic skills and offers us a valuable set of tools to increase our effectiveness and, thus, the magical quality of our own therapeutic work.

If you wish either to understand more about the language exchange in the therapeutic encounter or to increase the effectiveness and magical quality of your therapeutic work, *The Structure of Magic* offers a viable way to proceed. Magic is hidden in the language we speak. The webs that you can tie and untie are at your command if only you pay attention to what you already have (language) and the structure of the incantations for growth which we present in the remainder of this book.

FOOTNOTES FOR CHAPTER 1

1. In fact, part of what we will establish in the course of this book is that expressions such as *the right approach* or *the most powerful approach* are incomplete expressions. The questions that come to mind that we would ask to get the material to make the expressions complete are: *approach to what? right for whom? most powerful compared with what? most powerful for what purpose?* We have also provided a glossary of terms. We invite you to use it whenever you encounter a new or unfamiliar term.

2. We want to point out that we find this division (of the way that the model that each of us creates of the world will necessarily differ from the world) into three categories useful for our purposes of presenting the discussion of modeling by human beings. We are not suggesting that these three categories of differences are the only ones, or correct ones, or an exhaustive way of understanding the process of modeling. Furthermore, we are not suggesting that these three categories can be usefully distinguished from one another in all cases. Rather, consistent with the principles of modeling we are presenting, we find it useful for understanding the process of modeling itself.

3. We adopt this unusual terminology — *social genetics* — to remind the reader that social constraints on the behavior of members of society have as profound effect on shaping their perceptions as do neurological constraints.

Also, that neurological constraints, initially genetically determined, are subject to challenge and change just as are constraints initially socially determined. For example, the dramatic success which researchers have had in gaining voluntary control over portions of the so-called involuntary nervous system in humans (e.g., alpha wave) as well as in other species shows that neurological constraints are challengeable.

4.   This is only one of the more obvious ways in which languages shape the habitual perceptions of native speakers (Grinder and Elgin, 1972, pp. 6-7, and the writings of Benjamin Whorf and Edward Sapir). An annotated bibliography is also provided at the end of this book.

5.   Actually, from a purely linguistic point of view, the Maidu language has only two words to describe the color spectrum, *lak* and *tit*. The third word presented in the text is complex, having two meaningful parts or morphemes:

tu — urine and *lak* — red

We are interested, however, not in the results of a linguistic analysis, but rather in the habitual perceptions of the native speaker of Maidu. William Shipley, of the University of California, Santa Cruz, provided the Maidu information.

6.   Those of you who have learned to speak more than one language fluently will notice how your perception of the world and of yourself shifts when you shift from one language to the other.

7.   This has been clearly recognized by people like Gregory Bateson and R. D. Laing in their work on the schizophrenic family. Readers of Sherlock Holmes will also recognize this as one of his principles.

8.   Again, we wish to point out that our categories do not impose any necessity on the structure of reality — we have found these categories useful in organizing our own thinking and actions, both in presenting this material and in therapy; that is, in developing our model for therapy. We suspect that most readers will, if they think about the usual meanings of the terms, come to see Generalization and Deletion as special cases of Distortion.

Chapter 2

THE STRUCTURE OF LANGUAGE

One way in which human beings distinguish themselves from other animals is by the creation and use of language. The importance of language in coming to understand the history and present situation of the human race cannot be overestimated. As Edward Sapir has expressed it:

> The gift of speech and a well-ordered language are characteristic of every known group of human beings. No tribe has ever been found which is without language, and all statements to the contrary may be dismissed as mere folklore. There seems to be no warrant whatever for the statement which is sometimes made that there are certain people whose vocabulary is so limited that they cannot get on without the supplementary use of gesture, so that intelligible communication between members of such a group becomes impossible in the dark. The truth of the matter is that language is essentially perfect of expression and communication among every known people. Of all aspects of culture, it is a fair guess that language was the first to receive a highly perfected form and that its essential perfection is a prerequisite to the development of culture as a whole.
>
> Edward Sapir, *Culture, Language and Personality*, by D. Mandelbaum, (ed.)

All the accomplishments of the human race, both positive and negative, have involved the use of language. We as human beings use our language in two ways. We use it first of all to represent our experience — we call this activity reasoning, thinking, fantasying, rehearsing. When we are using language as a representational system, we are creating a model of our experience. This model of the world which we create by our representational use of language is based upon our perceptions of the world. Our perceptions are also partially determined by our model or representation in the ways we discussed in Chapter 1.

Notice that, since we use language as a representational system, our linguistic representations are subject to the three universals of human modeling: Generalization, Deletion, and Distortion. Secondly, we use our language to communicate our model or representation of the world to each other.[1] When we use our language to communicate, we call it talking, discussing, writing, lecturing, singing. When we are using our language for communication, we are presenting our model to others. This book, for example, presents a partial model of our experiences in therapy.

When humans communicate — when we talk, discuss, write — we usually are not conscious of the process of selecting words to represent our experience. We are almost never conscious of the way in which we order and structure the words we select. Language so fills our world that we move through it as a fish swims through water. Although we have little or no consciousness of the way in which we form our communication, our activity — the process of using language — is highly structured. For example, if you select any sentence in this book and reverse the order of the words in that sentence, or number the words 1, 2, 3, and move every odd word to the right over the even numbered word next to it, the sequence of words you are left with is nonsense. By destroying the structure of the sentence, it no longer makes sense; it no longer represents a model of any experience. Take this last sentence as a demonstration example.

Original version:

> *By destroying the structure of the sentence, it no longer makes sense; it no longer represents a model of any experience.*

After reversing the word order:[2]

> **Experience any of model a represents longer no it; sense makes longer no it, sentence the of structure the destroying by.*

After moving every odd numbered word to the right over the even numbered words:

> **Destroying by structure the the of it sentence, longer no sense; makes no it represents longer model a any of experience.*

To say that our communication, our language, is a system is to say that it has structure, that there is some set of rules which identify which sequences of words will make sense, will represent a model of our experience. In other words, our behavior when creating a representation or when communicating is rule-governed behavior. Even though we are not normally aware of the structure in the process of representation and communication, that structure, the structure of language, can be understood in terms of regular patterns.

Fortunately, there is a group of academicians who have made the discovery and explicit statement of these patterns the subject of their discipline — transformational grammar. In fact, transformational grammarians have developed the most complete and sophisticated explicit model of human, rule-governed behavior. The notion of human, rule-governed behavior is the key to understanding the way in which we as humans use our language.

> We can be fairly sure that a child has some rule system if his production [of sentences and phrases — JTG] is regular, if he extends these regularities to new instances, and if he can detect deviations from regularity in his own speech and the speech of others. This is, generally, what psycholinguists mean when they speak of the child's learning, or forming, or possession of linguistic rules. Note that I have left out the most stringent test for the existence of rules, namely: Can the individual state the explicit rule? ... Explicit statement of rules is irrelevant to our concerns here and is an entirely different sort of ability than we are considering here. As Susan Ervin-Tripp has put it:
>
>> To qualify as a native speaker ... one must learn ... rules. ... This is to say, of course, that one must learn to behave *as though one knew the rules.*
>>
>> (Slobin, 1967, p. x)
>
> What this means from the point of view of the scientific observer is that it is possible to describe the speaker's behavior in terms of rules. Such a description, however, should not be taken to imply that the particular rules devised by the scientist are actual entities existing inside the individual in a definite psychological or physiological sense.
>
> (Slobin, *Psycholinguistics*, Scott, Foreman & Co., 1971, p. 55)

The linguist's objective is to develop a grammar — a set of rules — which states what the well-formed patterns for any particular language are. This discipline is based on the brilliant work of Noam Chomsky, who initially developed a methodology and set of formal models for natural language.[3] As a result of the work of Chomsky and other transformationalists, it has been possible to develop a formal model for describing the regular patterns in the way we communicate our model of our experience. We use language to represent and communicate our experience — language is a model of our world. What transformational grammarians have done is to develop a formal model of our language, a model of our model of our world, or, simply, a Meta-model.

THE META-MODEL FOR LANGUAGE

Language serves as a representational system for our experiences. Our possible experiences as humans are tremendously rich and complex. If language is adequately to fulfill its function as a representational system, it must itself provide a rich and complex set of expressions to represent our possible experiences. Transformational grammarians have recognized that to approach the study of natural language systems by directly studying this rich and complex set of expressions would make their task overwhelming. They have chosen to study not the expressions themselves, but the rules for forming these expressions (syntax). Transformational grammarians make the simplifying assumption that the rules for forming this set of rich expressions can be studied independently of content.[4] For example, people who speak English as their native language make a consistent distinction between:

(1) *Colorless green ideas sleep furiously.*
(2) **Furiously sleep ideas green colorless.*

Even though there is something peculiar about the first group of words, people recognize that it is grammatical or well formed in some way that the second group of words is not. What we are demonstrating here is that people have consistent intuitions about the language they speak. By consistent intuitions, we mean that the same person presented with the same group of words today and a year from now will make the same judgments about whether they are a well-formed sentence of his language. Furthermore, different native speakers will make the same judgments about whether the same group of words is a sentence or not. These abilities are a classic example of human, rule-governed behavior. Although we are not conscious of *how* we are able to behave consistently, nevertheless, we do.

Transformational grammarians have created a model which

represents that rule-governed behavior — those consistent intuitions about sentences. The formal model in linguistics provides a solution to whether a particular group of words is a sentence or not, for example. The transformational model represents other kinds of linguistic intuitions also. Since the model is a description of human, rule-governed behavior, the way that we determine whether the rules of the model, fit or not is by checking them against the intuitions of the native speakers — intuitions available to every native speaker.

SOME UNIVERSALS OF THE HUMAN LINGUISTIC PROCESS

In Chapter 1, we discussed the three major processes of human modeling — Generalization, Deletion, and Distortion — three ways in which the model which we create will differ from the thing which it models. These processes apply, of course, with full force in the case of linguistic representations. Seen from this point of view, a large portion of the work which has been done by transformational linguists is the discovery and explicit statement of the way these three universals of representation are realized in the case of human language systems. Our ability and experience in using our language system to represent and communicate is so extensive that we are able to reflect on the process itself to the extent that we have consistent intuitions about that process. The purpose of the transformational model of language is to represent the patterns in the intuitions that we have about our language system. These intuitions are available to every native speaker of every language. The three major categories of linguistic intuitions which we have selected as relevant for our purposes are: Well-formedness, Constituent Structure, and Logical Semantic Relations.

I. **Well-Formedness:** The consistent judgments which native speakers make about whether or not groups of words are sentences of their language. Consider the following three groups of words:

(3) *Even the president has tapeworms.*
(4) *Even the president has green ideas.*
(5) *Even the president have tapeworms.*

The first is identified as well formed; that is, it conveys a meaning to the native speakers and they recognize it as being syntactically well formed; (2) is semantically ill formed; that is, it communicates no meaning that the native speaker recognizes as possible; (3) is syntactically ill formed although we may be able to assign some meaning to it.

II. **Constituent Structure:** The consistent judgments that native speakers make about what goes together as a unit or constituent inside a sentence of their language. For example, in the sentence

    (6) *The Guru of Ben Lomond thought Rosemary was at the controls.*

the words *The* and *Guru* go together in some way as a unit that *Guru* and *of* do not. These smaller level constituents go to make up larger units; for example, *The Guru* and *of Ben Lomond* go together in some way that *of Ben Lomond* and *was* do not.

III. **Logical Semantic Relations:** The consistent judgments which native speakers make about the logical relations reflected in the sentences of their language.

    1. *Completeness:* Native speakers, when presented with a verb of their language, are able to determine how many and what kinds of things between which this verb connects or describes a relationship. For example, the verb *kiss* in English implies a person kissing and a person or thing being kissed. The verb *hit* implies a person or thing hitting, a person or thing being hit, and an instrument being used for the hitting.

    2. *Ambiguity:* Native speakers recognize that a single sentence such as

        (7) *Investigating FBI agents can be dangerous.*

                or

        (8) *Maxine took Max's shirt off.*

    communicates two distinct meanings. Sentence (7) can be understood to mean either:

        (9) *FBI agents who are conducting investigations can be dangerous.*

                or

        (10) *To investigate FBI agents is possibly dangerous.*

    In sentence (8), it is unclear whether Maxine was wearing Max's shirt and took it off herself or she took Max's shirt off Max himself.

    3. *Synonymy:* Native speakers recognize that both of the following sentences have the same meaning or convey the same message.

        (11) *Sandy looked up the number.*

(12) *Sandy looked the number up.*
4. *Referential Indices:* Native speakers can determine whether a word or phrase picks out a particular object in their experience such as *my car* or whether it identifies a class of objects: *cars.* Furthermore, they make consistent judgments about whether two (or more) words refer to the same object or class, e.g., the words *Jackson* and *himself* in the sentence
(13) *Jackson changed himself.*
5. *Presuppositions:* Native speakers can determine what the experience of the speaker is for him to say a sentence. For example, if I say the sentence
(14) *My cat ran away.*
you are entitled (have reason) to believe that, in my experience of the world, it's true that
(15) *I have a cat.*

These three general categories of intuitions that human beings have about their language are represented explicitly in the transformational model.

THE TRANSFORMATIONAL MODEL

We will describe how the consistent intuitions we identified about our language are represented in the Meta-model — the model of transformational grammar.

Linguists using this model work to represent these intuitions which are available to every native speaker in an explicit way. Native speakers have two kinds of consistent intuitions about every sentence of their language. They are able to determine how the smaller units, such as words, go together to make up the sentence (intuitions about constituent structure) and also what a complete representation of the sentence would be (the completeness of the logical representation). For example, when presented with a sentence:

(16) *The woman bought a truck.*
a native speaker can group the words into constituents or larger level units such as:

/The woman/ and /bought/ and /a truck/
They will, in turn, group these units into
/The woman/ and /bought a truck/
The linguist represents these intuitions about what goes together inside a sentence by placing words which form a constituent (such

as *the* and *woman*) in what linguists call a tree structure which looks like:

The rule is that words which we as native speakers group into a single constituent are attached to the same point or node in the tree structure. The tree structure representation for (16) is:

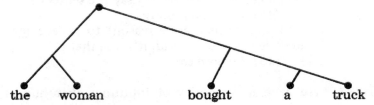

This is called the Surface Structure.

The second kind of consistent intuitions that native speakers have about a sentence such as (16) is what a complete representation of its meaning or logical semantic relation would be. One way which these intuitions are represented is:

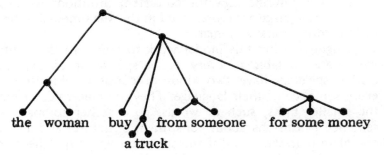

This is called the Deep Structure.

We are demonstrating how, within the transformational model, each sentence is analyzed at two levels of structure corresponding to two consistent kinds of intuitions which native speakers have: Surface Structure — in which their intuitions about constituent structure are given a tree structure representation — and Deep Structure — in which their intuitions, about what a complete representation of the logical semantic relations is, are given. Since the model gives two representations for each sentence (Surface

Structure and Deep Structure), linguists have the job of stating explicitly how these two levels are connected. The way in which they represent this connection is a process or derivation which is a series of transformations.

What Transformations Are

A transformation is an explicit statement of one kind of pattern which native speakers recognize among the sentences of their language. For example, compare the two sentences:

(17) *The woman bought the truck.*
(18) *The truck was bought by the woman.*

Native speakers recognize that, although these Surface Structures are different, the message communicated, or Deep Structures, of these two sentences is the same. The process by which these two sentences are derived from their common Deep Structure is called a derivation. A derivation is a series of transformations which connects the Deep Structure and the Surface Structure. The derivation of one of these two Surface Structures includes the transformation called the Passive Transformation. If you examine (17) and (18), you will notice that the order of the words is different. Specifically, the phrases *the woman* and *the truck* have been transposed. Transformational grammarians state this pattern as:

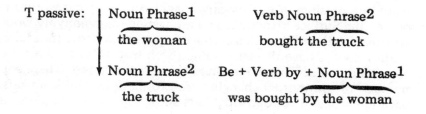

where the symbol ⏤ means "can be transformed into"

Notice that the statement of this pattern is not limited to just the two sentences (17) and (18), but is general in English:

(19) a. *Susan followed Sam.*
   b. *Sam was followed by Susan.*
(20) a. *The tapeworm ate the president.*
   b. *The president was eaten by the tapeworm.*
(21) a. *The bee touched the flower.*
   b. *The flower was touched by the bee.*

This is a simple example of how two Surface Structures whose derivations differ by only one transformation — the Passive Transformation applied in the derivation of the (b) versions, but not the (a) versions — are formed. Derivations can be much more complex; for example:

(22) a. *Timothy thought that Rosemary was guiding the spaceship.*

b. *The spaceship was thought by Timothy to have been guided by Rosemary.*

What all these pairs of sentences demonstrate is that Deep Structures may differ from their related Surface Structures by having the elements or words occur in a different order. Notice that in each pair of sentences, although the word order is different, the meaning appears to be constant. For each pair of sentences which have the same meaning, but different word orders, the linguist states a transformation which specifies exactly the pattern — the way the word order may differ.

Thus, the way that the native speaker's intuition of synonymy is represented is by stating a transformation which relates the two or more Surface Structures which are synonymous or have the same meaning. For each set of two or more Surface Structures which are synonymous, therefore, the transformational linguist states what the formal patterning is — the transformation. The test for synonymy intuitively is to attempt to imagine whether it would be possible in our (or any imaginary) consistent world that one of the Surface Structures you are testing for synonymy would be true (false) and the other Surface Structure not true (not false). If they always have the same value (both true or both false), they are synonymous. This is known as the paraphrase test. There are a number of word-order-changing transformations which linguists have identified. The following pairs show some of these patterns:

(23) a. *I want Borsch.*

b. *Borsch, I want.*

(24) a. *It is easy to scare Barry.*

b. *Barry is easy to scare.*

(25) a. *George gave Martha an apple.*

b. *George gave an apple to Martha.*

(26) a. *The Watergate 500 stumbled away.*

b. *Away stumbled the Watergate 500.*

(27) a. *Writing this sentence is easy.*

b. *It is easy to write this sentence.*

Each of these transformations specifies a way in which word orders can differ, and as a group are called Permutation Transformations.

Permutation Transformations are one of the two major classes of transformations; the other is called Deletion Transformations. For example:

(28) a. *Ilene talked to someone a great deal.*
       b. *Ilene talked a great deal.*

In the (b) version of (28), one of the Noun Phrases (i.e., *to someone*) has been deleted or removed. The general transformation which states this pattern is called Indefinite Noun Phrase Deletion.

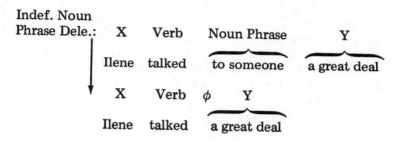

where X and Y are cover symbols or variables for any word(s) in those positions

Once again, there are a number of deletion transformations which linguists have identified:

(29) a. *Fluffo went to the store and Tab went to the store too.*
       b. *Fluffo went to the store and Tab went too.*
(30) a. *Tripod ate something.*
       b. *Tripod ate.*
(31) a. *Natural struck the wall with something.*
       b. *Natural struck the wall.*

In each of these pairs, the process or derivation of the second version includes a transformation which has deleted part of the complete logical semantic representation which is present in Deep Structure. Again, the meaning appears to remain the same even as elements of the Deep Structure are deleted.

Linguists distinguish two types of deletion transformations — Free Deletion, or deletion of indefinite elements, and Identity Deletion. Notice in the example pairs:

> *Ilene talked to someone a great deal.*
> *Ilene talked a great deal.*
> *Tripod ate something.*
> *Tripod ate.*
> *Natural struck the wall with something.*
> *Natural struck the wall.*

the element which has been deleted is an indefinite phrase *(to someone, something, with something)*, while in the example pair:

> *Fluffo went to the store and Tab went to the store too.*
> *Fluffo went to the store and Tab went too.*

a phrase which is definite *(to the store)* has been deleted. The general rule is that indefinite elements may be deleted from any sentence. There are special conditions which must be met before a definite element may be deleted. Notice, for example, the definite element *to the store,* which was legitimately deleted in the last sentence pair, occurs twice in that sentence, with the result that, after the deletion has occurred [(b) portion], one copy of the element is still present and no information has been lost.

Thus, Surface Structures may differ from their associated Deep Structure in two major ways:

- *The words may occur in a different order — Permutation Transformation*
- *Parts of the complete logical semantic representation may fail to appear in Surface Structure — Deletion Transformation.*

One additional way in which Deep Structure representation may differ from the Surface Structures which represent them is by the process of Nominalization. Essentially, the process of nominalization occurs when the transformations of the language change what occurs in the Deep Structure representation as a process word — a verb or predicate — into an event word — a noun or argument — in the Surface Structure representation. For example, compare the (a) and (b) versions of the following pairs of sentences:

(32) a. *Susan knows that she fears her parents.*
     b. *Susan knows her fear of her parents.*
(33) a. *Jeffery recognizes that he hates his job.*
     b. *Jeffery recognizes his hatred of his job.*
(34) a. *Debbie understands that she decides her own life.*
     b. *Debbie understands her decision about her own life.*

In the second version of each of the three pairs, what occurs in the first version as a verb or process word appears as a noun or event word. Specifically,

fears ⟶ fear

hates ⟶ hatred

decides ⟶ decision

Both Deletion and Permutation transformations may participate in this complex transformational process. For example, if permutation transformations had applied in the above nominalizations, we would have:

    (32) c. *Susan knows the fear by her of her parents.*
    (33) c. *Jeffery recognizes the hatred by him of his job.*
    (34) c. *Debbie understands the decision by her about her life.*

If, however, Deletion transformations had applied[5] in the above nominalizations, we would have the Surface Structure representations:

    (32) d. *Susan knows the fear.*
    (33) d. *Jeffery recognizes the hatred.*
    (34) d. *Debbie understands the decision.*

Whether Nominalization occurs with or without Deletion and Permutation transformations, its effect is to convert the Deep Structure representation of a process into the Surface Structure representation of an event.

What is important in this presentation is not the technical details nor the terminology that linguists have developed, but rather the fact that the intuitions available to each of us as a native speaker can be given a representation. Thus, the process of representation is itself represented. For example, the two major ways in which what we accept as a well-formed sentence can differ from its complete semantic representation is by distortion (Permutation Transformation or Nominalization) or removal of material (Deletion Transformation). As an example, each person who speaks English is able to consistently decide which groups of English words are well-formed sentences. This information is available to each of you. The transformational model represents this information. Thus, in the model, a group of words is said to be well formed if there is a series of transformations which convert the complete representation of Deep Structure into some Surface Structure.

Referential indices are involved in the transformational model in one important way for our purposes. Deletion Transformations are sensitive to referential indices. As mentioned previously, words or noun phrases may not be legitimately deleted by a Free deletion transformation if they bear a referential index which connects them to some person or thing. This shows up as a change in meaning if this condition is not met and the transformation is applied. Notice the difference between:

(35) a. *Kathleen laughed at someone.*
b. *Kathleen laughed.*
(36) a. *Kathleen laughed at her sister.*
b. *Kathleen laughed.*

The (b) version of (35) is understood to mean roughly the same thing as the (a) version, but the (b) version of (36) conveys less information and means something different. This example shows the general condition which a Free deletion transformation must meet to apply legitimately — that the element being deleted may not have a referential index which connects to some specific part of the speaker's model of his experience. In effect, this means that each time a Free deletion transformation has applied the deleted element necessarily had no referential index in the Deep Structure representation — that is, it was an element which is not connected to anything in the experience of the speaker.

In addition to the way that referential indices interact with the set of Deletion transformations, we as native speakers have full intuitions about their general use. Specifically, each of us as a native speaker can consistently distinguish words and phrases such as *this page, the Eiffel Tower, the Vietnam War, I, the Brooklyn Bridge, . . .* which have a referential index from words and phrases such as *someone, something, everyplace that there is trouble, all the people who didn't know me, it, . . .* which do not have a referential index. The first set of words and phrases identifies specific portions of the speaker's model of his experience while the second group does not. This second group of words and phrases without a referential index is one of the major ways in which the modeling process of Generalization is realized in natural language systems.

In recent work in linguistics, transformationalists have begun to explore how presuppositions work in natural language. Certain sentences imply that certain other sentences must be true in order for them to make sense. For example, if I hear you say:

(37) *There is a cat on the table.*

I may choose to believe that there is a cat on the table or not and, either way, I can make sense out of what you are saying. However, if I hear you say:

(38) *Sam realized that there is a cat on the table.*

I must assume that there is, in fact, a cat on the table in order to make any sense out of what you are saying. This difference shows up clearly if I introduce the negative element *not* into the sentence.

(39) *Sam doesn't realize that there is a cat on the table.*

This shows that when one says the sentence which means the opposite — the one that denies what the first one claims is true — one still must assume that there is a cat on the table in order to make sense out of the sentence. A sentence which must be true in order for some other sentence to make sense is called the presupposition of the second sentence.

AN OVERVIEW

The parts of the transformational model relevant for our purposes have been presented. Viewed together, they constitute a representation of the process that humans go through in representing their experience and communicating that representation. When humans wish to communicate their representation, their experience of the world, they form a complete linguistic representation of their experience; this is called the Deep Structure. As they begin to speak, they make a series of choices (transformations) about the form in which they will communicate their experience. These choices are not, in general, conscious choices.

> The structure of a sentence can be viewed as the result of a series of syntactic choices made in generating it. The speaker encodes meaning by choosing to build the sentence with certain syntactic features, chosen from a limited set.
>
> (T. Winograd, *Understanding Natural Language*, p. 16, in Cognitive Psychology, Vol. 3, no. 1, Jan., 1972)

Our behavior in making these choices is, however, regular and rule governed. The process of making this series of choices (a derivation) results in a Surface Structure — a sentence or sequence of words which we recognize as a well-formed group of words in our language. This Surface Structure itself can be viewed as a representation of the full linguistic representation — the Deep Structure. The transformations change the structure of the Deep Structure — either deleting or changing the word order — but do not change the semantic meaning. Graphically, the entire process can be viewed as: (See top of page 36)

The model of this process is a model of what we do when we represent and communicate our model — a model of a model — a

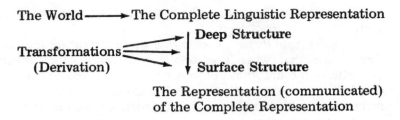

The Representation (communicated)
of the Complete Representation

Meta-model. This Meta-model represents our intuitions about our experience. For example, our intuition of synonymy — the case in which two or more Surface Structures have the same semantic meaning, i.e., the same Deep Structure — is represented as:

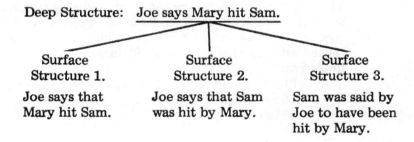

In terms of a specific example, then:

Deep Structure: Joe says Mary hit Sam.

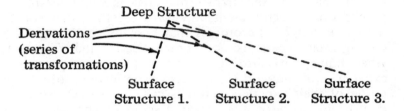

Surface Structure 1.	Surface Structure 2.	Surface Structure 3.
Joe says that Mary hit Sam.	Joe says that Sam was hit by Mary.	Sam was said by Joe to have been hit by Mary.

Synonymy in the Meta-model means that the same Deep Structure is connected with more than one Surface Structure.

Ambiguity is the opposite case. Ambiguity is the intuition that native speakers use when the same Surface Structure has more than one distinct semantic meaning and is represented as: (See top of page 37)

Ambiguity in the Meta-model is the case wherein more than one Deep Structure is connected by transformations with the same Surface Structure.

The intuition of well-formedness is represented in the Meta-model in that any sequence of words is well formed just in case

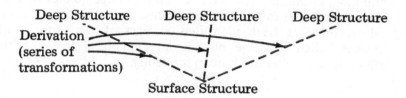

As a specific example:

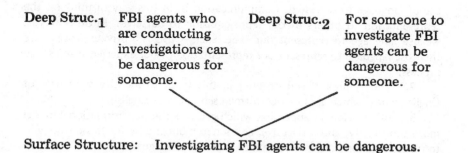

Deep Struc.$_1$ FBI agents who are conducting investigations can be dangerous for someone.

Deep Struc.$_2$ For someone to investigate FBI agents can be dangerous for someone.

Surface Structure: Investigating FBI agents can be dangerous.

---

there is a series of transformations (a derivation) which carries some Deep Structure into that sequence of words — a Surface Structure. Thus, the Meta-model is an explicit representation of our unconscious, rule-governed behavior.

SUMMARY

Human language is a way of representationing the world. Transformational Grammar is an explicit model of the process of representing and of communicating that representation of the world. The mechanisms within Transformational Grammar are universal to all human beings and the way in which we represent our experience. The semantic meaning which these processes represent is existential, infinitely rich and varied. The way in which these existential meanings are represented and communicated is rule governed. Transformational Grammar models not the existential meaning, but the way that infinite set is formed — the rules of representations themselves.

The nervous system which is responsible for producing the representational system of language is the same nervous system by which humans produce every other model of the world —

thinking, visual, kinistic, etc. . . . The same principles of structure are operating in each of these systems. Thus, the formal principles which linguists have identified as part of the representational system called language provide an explicit approach to understanding any system of human modeling.

FOOTNOTES FOR CHAPTER 2

1.   This use of language to communicate is actually a special case of the use of language to represent. Communication is, in this way of thinking, the representation to others of our representation to ourselves. In other words, we use language to represent our experience — this is a private process. We then use language to represent our representation of our experience — a social process.

2.   The symbol * will be used in this book to identify sequences of English words which are not well-formed sentences of English.

3.   We provide an appendix, which presents the transformational model more thoroughly, and a selective, annotated bibliography for those who wish to further examine the transformational model of language.

4.   This is not true of all linguists who may refer to themselves as transformationalists. The present split in the field — Extended Standard Theorists and Generative Semanticists — is not relevant for our purposes in adapting certain portions of the Transformational model for our Meta-model for therapy. The recent work, especially by people in Generative Semantics, will be useful, we believe, in expanding the Meta-model we present here. See the bibliography for sources.

5.   Strictly speaking, the deletion of the elements deleted in the text is not legitimate from a purely linguistic point of view, as they are carrying referential indices — the process, however, is typical of clients in therapy.

Chapter 3

THE STRUCTURE OF MAGIC

One of the mysteries in the field of therapy is that, although the various schools of therapy have very different forms, they all succeed to some degree. This puzzle will be solved when the effective methods shared by the different psychotherapies can be described in a single set of terms, thus making the similarities explicit and thereby learnable by therapists of any school.[1]

> ... this list of similarities [among the various forms of psychotherapy — RB/JG] is hardly comprehensive; there would seem to be sufficient indication that a more thorough study of all forms of psychotherapy in terms of their similar formal patterns would be rewarding. A more rigorous science of psychotherapy will arrive when the procedures in the various methods can be synthesized down to the most effective strategy possible to induce a person to spontaneously behave in a different matter.
>
> J. Haley, *Strategies of Psychotherapy*, 1967, p. 85.

The one feature that is present in all forms of therapy when they are successful is that the people in therapy change in some way. This change is given different names by different schools of therapy, such as: 1) fixing, 2) cure, 3) growth, 4) enlightenment, 5) behavior modification, etc. Whatever the name given the phenomenon, it somehow makes the person's experience richer and better. This is not surprising as every form of therapy claims to help people operate more successfully in the world. When people change, their experience and model of the world is different. No matter what their techniques, the different forms of therapy make it possible for people to change their model of the world and some make part of that model new.

What we are offering here is not a new school of therapy, but rather a specific set of tools/techniques which are an explicit representation of what is already present to some degree in each form of therapy. The unique aspects of the Meta-model we are presenting are: first, that it is based on the intuitions already available to every native speaker, and second, it is an explicit model in that it is learnable.

THE META-MODEL

The Meta-model we are presenting is in large part inspired by the formal model developed in transformational linguistics. Since the transformational model was created to answer questions which are not immediately connected with the way that humans change, not all portions of it are equally useful in creating a Meta-model for therapy. Thus, we have adapted the model, selecting only the portions relevant for our purposes and arranging them in a system appropriate for our objectives in therapy.

In this chapter, we will present our Meta-model for therapy. Here, our intention is to give you an overall picture of what is available in the Meta-model and how it works. In the two succeeding chapters, we become specific, showing you in a step-by-step format how to apply the Meta-model techniques. For this chapter, we urge you to read through the discussion and attempt to get the overall image we present. We will sharpen and detail that image in the following chapters.

Deletions: The Missing Parts of the Model

In most forms of therapy (with the possible exclusion of some physical therapies) one of the things that goes on is a series of verbal transactions between the "client" and the "therapist." One of the common features of the therapeutic encounter is that the therapist tries to find out what the client has come to therapy for; what the client wants to change. In our terms, the therapist is attempting to find out what model of the world the client has. As clients communicate their models of the world, they do it in Surface Structures. These Surface Structures will contain deletions such as those described in the last chapter. The way that the client uses language to communicate his model/representation is subject to the universal processes of human modeling such as deletion.

The Surface Structure itself is a representation of the full linguistic representation from which it is derived — the Deep Structure. In the case wherein the linguistic process of deletion has occurred, the resulting verbal description — the Surface Structure — is necessarily missing for the therapist. This piece may also be missing from the client's conscious model of the world. If the model of the client's experience has pieces missing, it is impoverished. Impoverished models, as we stated before, imply limited options for behavior. As the missing pieces are recovered, the process of change in that person begins.

The first step is for the therapist to be able to determine whether the client's Surface Structure is a complete representation of the full linguistic representation from which it is derived — the Deep Structure. At this point in time, therapists either have a highly developed sense of intuitions based upon their experiences or they may use the explicit Meta-model to recover the missing pieces. In the Meta-model, the intuitions, which every native speaker of the language has, come into play. The client says:

I'm scared.

The therapist now checks his (or her) intuitions to determine whether the client's Surface Structure is complete. One way of doing this (we present this process in detail in the following chapters) is to ask yourself whether you can think of another well-formed sentence in English which has the same process word *scare* and more noun arguments than the client's Surface Structure with that same verb *scare*. If you can think of such a Surface Structure, then the client's Surface Structure is incomplete.

Therapists are now faced with three broad options.[2] They may accept the impoverished model, they may ask for the missing piece, or they may guess at it. The first option, accepting the impoverished model, presents the difficulty of making the process of therapy slow and tedious, as it places total responsibility for recovering the model's missing pieces on the client, who is there for assistance in this process in the first place. We are not suggesting that change is not possible in this process, but that it requires a longer period of time than is necessary. The second choice is for the therapist to ask for the piece that has been linguistically deleted:

C: *I'm scared.*
T: *Of what?*

Either the client supplies the material in his model that has been linguistically deleted and the therapist's understanding of that model becomes more complete, or the piece missing from the client's verbal expression is also missing from his model. Clients begin the process of self-discovery and change as they begin to work to fill in the missing pieces and become actively involved in this process of self-discovery — expanding themselves by expanding their model of the world.

Therapists have a third choice — they may, from long experience, have an intuition about what the missing piece is. They may choose to interpret or guess at the missing piece. We have no quarrel with this choice. There is, however, the danger that any form of interpretation or guessing may be inaccurate. We include a safeguard for the client in our Meta-model. The client tries the interpretation or guess by the therapist by generating a sentence which includes that material and checks his intuitions to see whether it fits, makes sense, is an accurate representation of his model of the world. For example, the therapist may have a strong intuition that the client is scared of his father. His intuition may be based upon previous therapy or upon his recognition of a particular body posture or movement he has seen the client use at other times when the subject of his father has come up. In this case, the exchange may go:

C: *I'm scared.*

T: *I want you to try saying this and see whether it fits for you: "My father scares me."*

What he is asking the client to do here is to say the Surface Structure containing his guess or interpretation and see whether it fits the client's full representation, the Deep Structure.[3] If this new Surface Structure containing the therapist's intuition about the identity of the deleted portion of the client's original Surface Structure fits the client's model, he will typically experience a certain sensation of congruity or recognition. If not, the Meta-model techniques are available as a guide for recovering the missing material which actually fits the client's model. The safeguard for the client's integrity is for the therapist to be sensitive to the client's intuitions and experience by having the client judge whether the therapist's guess is accurate for his model by saying the sentence and seeing whether it fits.

The need for therapists to be aware of the integrity of their clients has been widely recognized. Polster and Polster (1973, p. 68) comment:

> There is no precise yardstick to identify the limits of an individual's power to assimilate or express feelings which have explosive possibilities, but there is a basic safeguard — not forcing or seducing him into behaviors which he himself has not largely set up.

In general, the effectiveness of a particular form of therapy is associated with its ability to recover "suppressed" or missing pieces of the client's model. Thus, the first step in acquiring this set of tools is to learn to identify the pieces missing in the model — specifically, to identify the fact that linguistic deletion has occurred. The pieces that are missing in the Surface Structure are the material which has been removed by the Deletion Transformations. Recovering the missing material involves a movement toward a fuller representation — the Deep Structure.

Distortion: Process——►Event

One of the ways people become immobilized is to turn an ongoing process into an event. Events are things which occur at one point in time and are finished. Once they occur, their outcomes are fixed and nothing can be done to change them.[4] This way of representing their experience is impoverishing in the sense that clients lose control of ongoing processes by representing them as events. Linguists have identified the linguistic mechanism for turning a process into an event. This is called nominalization and is discussed in the last chapter. The therapist's ability to challenge the distorted portions of the client's model involving the representation of processes as events requires that the therapist be able to recognize nominalizations in the client's Surface Structures. This can be accomplished by examining the client's Surface Structure — check each of the non-verbs in the sentence, asking yourself whether you can think of a verb or adjective which is closely associated with it in appearance/sound and meaning. (Again, a more detailed procedure will be given in Chapter 4.) For example, as the client begins to discuss some ongoing process in his life — the continuing process of his deciding to avoid confronting someone about something — he may represent this process in his Surface Structure by the phrase *my decision:*

> *I really regret my decision.*

The therapist, checking for distortions, identifies the noun *decision* as being similar in appearance/sound and meaning to the process word *decide* — thus, a nominalization.

The task of the therapist is to help the client see that what he has represented in his model as a closed, finished event is an ongoing process which may be influenced by him. There are a number of ways of accomplishing this. For example, the therapist may ask how the client feels about his decision. When the client responds that he is dissatisfied, the therapist asks what it is that stops him from reconsidering his decision. The client responds, and the therapist continues to apply the techniques of the Meta-model. Here, the therapist is working to reconnect the event with the present process.

Another challenge the therapist may use is:

> *You have made your decision and there is nothing which you can imagine that would change your decision?*

Again, the client responds with a Surface Structure which the therapist may use, along with the Meta-model, as a guide to his next move in inducing change in the client.

The effect of systematically applying these two techniques:

  (a) Recovery of pieces removed by the deletion transformations from the Deep Structure.

  (b) Transformation of nominalizations back into process words they were derived from — the Deep Structure.

yields a fuller representation of the client's model — the linguistic Deep Structure from which the client's initial verbal expressions, or Surface Structures, were derived. This process actively involves the client in filling in the missing pieces and in turning things represented as events back into processes, thereby beginning the process of change.

Deep Structures are fullest linguistic representations of the client's experience. They may differ from that person's experience in a number of ways which are already familiar to you. These are the three features which are common to all human modeling processes: Deletion, Distortion, and Generalization. These are the universal processes of human modeling — the way that people create any representation of their experience.

The intuitions which are represented in the transformational model of language are special cases of these three principles; for example, sentences or Surface Structures which have no expressed subject are examples of the process of deletion. To develop an image of the model the client has, this missing piece has to be restored; the expression has to be reconnected with its source — its fullest representation. In the case of a Surface Structure, its source and fullest representation is the Deep Structure. In the case of the Deep Structure, the client's experiences are the source for the representation. While Deep Structure is the fullest linguistic representation, it is derived from a fuller, richer source — the sum total of the client's experiences.[5] Not surprisingly, the same universal processes of human modeling which give us a systematic way of assisting the client in going from an impoverished Surface Structure to a complete linguistic representation — the Deep Structure — provide a systematic way of connecting the linguistic representation for that person to the set of full experiences from which the full linguistic representation is derived.

Deep Structure and Beyond

As we have repeatedly pointed out, individuals who find themselves in therapy and wish help in changing are typically there because they feel that they do not have enough choices, that they are unable to behave other than they do. Furthermore, however peculiar their behavior may appear to us, it makes sense in their model of the world.

The therapist has succeeded in involving the client in recovering the Deep Structure — the full linguistic representation. The next step is to challenge that Deep Structure in such a way as to enrich it. The therapist has a number of choices at this point. The basic principle here is that people end up in pain, not because the world is not rich enough to allow them to satisfy their needs, but because their representation of the world is impoverished. Correspondingly, then, the strategy that we as therapists adopt is to connect the client with the world in some way which gives him a richer set of choices. In other words, since the client experiences pain by having created an impoverished representation of the world and forgetting that the representation is not the world, the therapist will assist the client in changing just in case he comes to behave in some way inconsistent with his model and thereby enriches his model. There are a number of ways of accomplishing this, many of which have been described in detail. The importance of clear sensory channels, the uncovering of patterns of coping with stress learned in the family system, the childhood traumas, the imposition of therapeutic double binds — are all examples of the emphases which the various forms of psychotherapy have selected as their way of challenging the client's impoverished model. Whatever the school of therapy and whatever its typical emphasis and form of treatment, when successful it characteristically involves two features:

(1) A large amount of communication in the form of language.[6]
(2) A change in the client's representation/model of the world.

What we offer in our Meta-model relates directly to both of these features of successful therapy. Language is both a representational system and the means or process of communicating our representation of the world. The processes which we go through to communicate our experience are the same processes which we go through in creating our experience. Seen in this way, the recovery of the full Deep Structure from the Surface Structure corresponds to the uncovering of the client's full linguistic model of the world; the challenge to the client's Deep Structure is directly a challenge to the client's full linguistic representation. The same tools/ techniques apply to both.

The processes by which people impoverish their representation of the world are the same processes by which they impoverish their expression of their representation of the world. The way that people have created pain for themselves involves these processes. Through them they have created an impoverished model. Our Meta-model offers a specific way to challenge these same processes to enrich their model. First, the Meta-model specifies the process of moving from Surface Structure to Deep Structure. The process of the moving from a Surface Structure with a deletion to the full Deep Structure not only provides the therapist with an accurate image of the client's model, but in the process the client may, in fact, expand the model in attempting to recover the deletion for which the therapist is asking. Second, it supplies a format for challenging the Deep Structure and reconnecting it with the person's experience, thus making change possible.

Having recovered the client's linguistic model of the world, the therapist may now select any one, or more than one, of a number of techniques of treatment which he feels useful in the context. The therapist may, for example, choose to impose a therapeutic double-bind (Haley, 1973) or to use an enactment technique (Perls, 1973), to assist in the process of change, or continue to challenge the client's model by purely verbal work. In each of these cases, language is involved. The effectiveness and potency of a therapist is intimately connected with the richness of his Meta-model — the number of choices he has and his skill in combining these options. Our focus in this work will be on the verbal/digital, not the non-verbal/analogical techniques, for two reasons:

(1) Verbal transactions are a significant form of communication in all styles of therapy.

(2) We have developed a model for natural language which is explicit.

We will show in detail later that the Meta-model which we have created from the Transformational Grammar model for a therapeutic Meta-model can be generalized to non-verbal systems of communication as well.[7]

Challenging Deep Structure

For the therapist to challenge the Deep Structure is equivalent to demanding that the client mobilize his resources to reconnect his linguistic model with his world of experience. In other words, the therapist here is challenging the client's assumptions that his linguistic model is reality.

Challenging Generalizations

One element that a client's model will possess which typically impoverishes his experience is that of generalization. Correspondingly, the Deep Structure which represents the impoverished portion of the model will contain words and phrases which have no referential index and verbs which are incompletely specified.

Clarity Out of Chaos — the Noun/Arguments

As the missing pieces of the client's Deep Structure are recovered, the model of the client's experience may become more complete, yet it may still be unclear and unfocused.[8] The client says:

> C: *I'm scared.*
> T: *Of what?*
> C: *Of people.*

At this point, the therapist either has a well-developed set of intuitions about what to do next or he may use our explicit Meta-model as a guide. One explicit way of determining which portions of the verbal expression (and the model it represents) are unfocused is to check for noun arguments that have no referential index. The therapist again has three basic choices: to accept the unfocused model, to ask a question which demands focusing of the model, or to guess what the focused model may be. The choice made by the therapist here has the same consequences as did his attempting to recover pieces missing in the model. If the therapist chooses to ask for the missing referential index, he simply says:

> *Who, specifically (scares you)?*

If, on the other hand, the therapist has an intuition about the identity of the noun phrase which has no referential index, he may decide to guess. In this case, the same way of safeguarding the client's integrity is available if the therapist chooses to guess.

> C: *I'm scared.*
> T: *Of what?*
> C: *Of people.*

The therapist decides to guess who it is who *specifically* scares the client. Employing the safeguard we recommend, the therapist asks the client to say the Surface Structure which incorporates the therapist's guess.

> T: *I want you to try saying this and see whether you feel it fits for you: "My father scares me."*

The client now says the Surface Structure incorporating the guess or interpretation and determines whether it fits his model. In either case, the therapist is responding — challenging the client's generalization by demanding that the client connect this generalization with his specific experience — by demanding a referential index. This, the next step in the process of the therapist's understanding the client's model, is the challenge to the noun arguments which have no referential index.

The word "people" does not pick out a specific individual or group of individuals in the client's model. The client may supply the referential index missing in the verbal expression and available in his model and the therapist's understanding of his model is thus more focused, or the referential index may be missing in the client's model also. If that portion of the client's model is also unfocused, the question by the therapist allows the client to work toward clarifying his model and to become more involved in the process.

Notice that the client may produce a number of responses such as "people who hate me," "all the people I always thought were my friends," "everyone I know," "some of my family," none of which have referential indices — they are intentional, not extensional, descriptions of the person's experience.[9] They represent generalizations which are still not connected to the client's experience. The therapist continues to challenge these formulations by asking:

Who, specifically?

until they get from the client a verbal expression which has a referential index. Finally, the client responds:

My father scares me.

The demand by the therapist for full Deep Structure representations which include only words and phrases which have referential indices is a demand that the client re-connect his generalizations with the experience from which they came. Next, the therapist asks himself whether the image he has of the client's model is clear and focused.

Clarity Out of Chaos — Verb/Process Words

Both the nouns in the verbal expression:

My father scares me.

have referential indices *(my father* and *me)*. The process word or verb in the expression, however, gives us no clear image of precisely how the experience took place. We know that the client is scared and that his father scares him, but how, exactly, his father scares him is incompletely represented — what, specifically, is it that he *does* which scares him. The therapist asks the client to focus his image by the question:

How does your father scare you?

This is again a request by the therapist for the client to connect his generalization to the experience from which it was derived. The answer to this question by the client is a new Surface Structure which the therapist now examines for completeness and clarity, asking himself whether all the portions of the full Deep Structure representation are reflected in that Surface Structure. The therapist continues to examine the Surface Structures generated by the client, recovering the Deep Structure and challenging the Deep Structure for generalizations which make the model unfocused and incompletely specified until the image that the therapist has of the client's model is clear.

Challenging Deletions

When human beings create their linguistic models of the world, they necessarily select and represent certain portions of the world and fail to select and represent others.[10] Thus, one way in which the full linguistic representation — the Deep Structure — will differ from the experience which it represents is by being a reduced version of the client's full experience of the world. This reduction may, as we said before, be a useful reduction, or it may impoverish the model in such a way that it creates pain for that person. The techniques available to the therapist to assist the client in recovering portions of his experience which he did not represent in his model are many. In the area of combined verbal—non-verbal techniques, for example, the client might be asked to enact the specific situation from which he generalized and to describe his experience fully as he re-lives it — thus presenting the portion of his experience to which he had failed previously to give a linguistic representation. This re-connects the client with his experience and simultaneously provides the therapist with valuable content as well as an understanding of how the person typically represents his experiences. Again, our intention in this study is to focus on the linguistic techniques.

The therapist's task is to challenge deletions which are not useful; those which cause pain are ones which are associated with areas of impossibility, areas in which the client literally cannot see any choices other than ones which are unsatisfactory — ones which are painful. Typically, an area in which an impoverishing deletion has occurred is one in which the client's perception of his potential is limited — he seems to be blocked, stuck, doomed. . . .

The technique of recovering the full linguistic representation works and it is learnable, as there exists an explicit representation — the Deep Structure — with which the Surface Structure can be compared. This is essentially the process of comparing a representation (Surface Structure) with the full model from which it was derived — the Deep Structure. The Deep Structures themselves are derived from the full range of experience available to human beings. The Deep Structure is available to any native speaker by intuition. The world of experience is available to anyone willing to experience it. As therapists, we identify as a deletion from the client's model any option which we can imagine that we would have, or anyone whom we know would have, in the same situation.

At this point, the deletion from the experience of the client's model of the world will often be so obvious to therapists that they may begin to offer suggestions/advice about alternative ways of dealing with the problem. It is likely we would agree with many of the suggestions made by the therapist, as our experience would include these alternatives, but, in our experience, suggestions or advice which fall into the gaps created by deletion in a client's model are relatively ineffective. These deletions have impoverished the client's model, and it is precisely those portions of the client's possible experience which the therapist is recommending that are not represented in the model. Here, typically, the client will either "resist" or not hear the options, as he has deleted them from his model. Thus, we suggest that the therapist keep these suggestions until the client's model is rich enough to incompass them.

An additional advantage to the therapist's withholding suggestions and involving the client in challenging his own model and creating his own solutions is that the therapist avoids becoming bogged down in content and is able to focus, instead, on the process of directing the client's coping. That is, the therapist uses his Meta-model to operate directly on the client's impoverished model.

We have identified a number of questions which are useful in assisting the client in expanding his model. When clients approach the limits of their models, they often say things such as:

> *I can't trust people.*
> *It's impossible for me to trust people.*

Now, since we as therapists know that either we ourselves have been able to trust others or we know someone who has succeeded in trusting someone else, we are aware that the world is rich enough to allow the client to come to trust people — it's that person's model which prevents it. The question for us then becomes: How is it that some people are able to trust others but our client is not? We get this directly by asking the client to explain the difference in his model which makes this impossible. That is, we ask:

> *What is it that stops you from trusting people?*

or

What would happen if you trusted people?

A full answer to this question by the client will restore some of the deleted material. The client, of course, will respond in some Surface Structure. The therapist has the tools available for evaluating these verbal responses — the processes of restoring the Deep Structure, of focusing portions of the image which are unclear. These same tools serve the therapist in assisting the client to change by re-connecting the client with his experience. The therapist has a goal, using the techniques of the Meta-model, to gain a clear, fully focused image of the client's model which has a rich set of choices for the client in the areas in which the client has pain. The use of the question:

What stops you from. . .?

is crucial in re-connecting the client to his experience in such a way as to give him access to material which was formerly deleted and, therefore, not represented in his model.

Distortion

By distortion, we refer to things which are represented in the client's model but are twisted in some way which limits his ability to act and increases his potential for pain. There are a number of ways in which the Deep Structure may be distorted from the world in such a way as to create pain.

Semantic Well-Formedness

One way in which people distort their model and cause themselves pain is by assigning outside of their control responsibilities which are within their control. Linguists have identified certain expressions semantically ill-formed. For example:

George forced Mary to weigh 114 pounds.

Their generalization is that people cannot legitimately be said to be able to cause other people to do things which are not within their voluntary control. We have generalized the notion of semantic ill-formedness to include sentences such as:

My husband makes me mad.

The therapist can identify this sentence as having the form:

Some person causes some person to have some emotion.

When the first person, the one doing the causing, is different from the person experiencing the anger, the sentence is said to be semantically ill-formed and unacceptable. The semantic ill-formedness of sentences of this type arises because it, literally, is not possible for one human being to create an emotion in another human being — thus, we reject sentences of this form. Sentences of this type, in fact, identify situations in which one person does some act and a second person *responds* by feeling a certain way. The point here is that, although the two events occur one after another, there is no necessary connection between the act of one person and the response of the other. Therefore, sentences of this type identify a model in which the client assigns responsibility for his emotions to people or forces outside his control. The act itself does not cause the emotion; rather, the emotion is a response generated from a model in which the client takes no responsibility for experiences which he *could* control.

The therapist's task at this point is to challenge the model in some way which assists clients in taking responsibility for their responses. This can be accomplished in a number of ways. The therapist may ask if she becomes angry every time her husband does what he does. The therapist has a number of choices at this point. For example, if the client maintains that she always becomes angry when her husband does this, the therapist may challenge that by asking how, specifically, he makes her angry. If, on the other hand, the client admits that sometimes her husband does what he does and she doesn't become angry, the therapist may ask her to identify what is different at the times that this act of her husband's fails to have its "automatic" effect. We will present these techniques in the next two chapters.

Again, these techniques will allow the therapist to re-connect the client with his experience and to untwist the limiting distortions.

Presuppositions

What may at first appear to us as therapists as bizarre behavior or peculiar statements by clients will make sense to us in their models. To have a clear image of the client's model is to understand how that behavior or those statements make sense. This is equivalent to identifying the assumptions that the client is making in his model of the world. Assumptions in a model show up linguistically as presuppositions of the client's sentences. Presuppositions are what is necessarily true for the statements that the client makes to make sense (not to be true, but just to be meaningful) at all. One short-cut method for therapists to identify the portions of the client's model which are impoverished is to be able to recognize the presuppositions of the client's sentences. The client states:

I realize that my wife doesn't love me.

The therapist may respond by identifying the presupposition and challenge it directly by bringing the presupposition of the Surface

Structure out into the open for examination and challenge. In order to understand the sentence at all, it is necessary for the therapist to accept the presuppositions:

Her husband doesn't love her.

There is an explicit test for what, if any, presuppositions a sentence has. The therapist takes the Surface Structure and forms a new sentence which is the same as the old one except that it has a negative word in it attached to the first verb — in this case the sentence:

I don't realize that my husband doesn't love me.

Then, the therapist simply asks himself whether the same sentence would have to be true in order for this new sentence to make sense. Any sentence which must be true for both the client's statement and the new statement, which was formed by the old statement plus the negative word, to make sense is a presupposition. Presuppositions are particularly insidious as they are not presented openly for consideration. They identify in the model some of the basic organizing principles which limit the client's experience.

Once the therapist has identified the presuppositions of the client's statements, he may challenge it directly by the techniques we have already identified in the Deletion Section.

SUMMARY

When therapy, whatever its form, is successful, it involves a change in the clients' models in some way which allows clients more choice in their behavior. The methods which we have presented in the Meta-model are effective in enriching a client's model of the world — which entails that some aspect of his model is new. It's important that this new portion of his model be solidly connected with his experience. To insure this, clients must actually exercise, practice, become familiar with, and experience their new choices. Most therapies have developed specific techniques for accomplishing this: e.g., psychodrama, homework, tasks, etc. The purpose of these techniques is to integrate the new aspect of his model into the client's experience.

OVERVIEW

Successful therapy involves change. The Meta-model, adapted from the transformational model of language, provides an explicit method for understanding and changing clients' impoverished models. One way to understand the overall effect of this Meta-model is in terms of well-formedness. As native speakers, we can consistently distinguish between groups of words which are well formed — i.e., sentences — and groups of words which are not well formed. That is, we can intuitively make the distinction between what is well formed in English and what is not. What we are proposing here is that there is a subset of the well-formed sentences of English which we recognize as well formed in therapy. This set, the set of sentences which are well formed in therapy and acceptable to us as therapists, are sentences which:

(1) Are well formed in English, and
(2) Contain no transformational deletions or unexplored deletions in the portion of the model in which the client experiences no choice.
(3) Contain no nominalizations (process $\longrightarrow$ event).
(4) Contain no words or phrases lacking referential indices.
(5) Contain no verbs incompletely specified.
(6) Contain no unexplored presuppositions in the portion of the model in which the client experiences no choice.
(7) Contain no sentences which violate the semantic conditions of well-formedness.

By applying these well-formedness conditions to the client's Surface Structures, the therapist has an explicit strategy for inducing change in the client's model.[11] Using these grammatical conditions appropriate for therapy, therapists enrich their model independently of the particular form of therapy they do. While this set of tools will greatly increase the potency of any form of therapy, we are aware that there is a great deal going on in the therapeutic encounter which is not solely digital (verbal). Rather, we are saying that the digital system is important, and we are offering an explicit Meta-model. The nervous system which produces digital communication (e.g., language) is the same nervous system which generates the other forms of human behavior which occur in the therapeutic encounter — analogical communication systems, dreams, etc. The remainder of this book is designed to accomplish two things: first, to familiarize you with the use of the Meta-model we have presented, and secondly, to show you how the general processes of the Meta-model for the digital can be generalized to these other forms of human behavior.

FOOTNOTES FOR CHAPTER 3

1. We highly recommend the excellent work by Jay Haley, Gregory Bateson and his associates, Paul Watlawick, Janet Beavin, and Don Jackson. Their studies appear to us to be, at present, the closest approximation along with the Meta-model to achieving this goal.

2. We are aware that the three options discussed here do not exhaust all the logical or, indeed, practical possibilities. The therapist could, for example, ignore completely the Surface Structure the client presents. The three categories of response by the therapist that we discuss seem to us to be the most frequent.

3. In Chapter 6 we will return to this technique under the general heading of *Congruity Technique.* Here, simply, the client, by uttering the Surface Structure, calls up the Deep Structure. If the Surface Structure corresponds to a Deep Structure which fits his model (is congruent with his model), the client will experience some recognition.

4. In Chapter 2, as well as in the remainder of the book, we adopt the standard philosophical linguistic view that only nouns in the Surface Structure which correspond to verbs in Deep Structure are the result of nominalizations: the change of the representation of a process into an event. A more radical view is that even Surface Structure nouns which, by the standard linguistic analysis, do not correspond to verbs in Deep Structure are the representation of a process by an event. In this view, the noun *chair* is the event representation of what we actually experience in the process of perception, manipulation, ... one which has space-time coordinates and duration. The difference, then, between parts of our experience which are represented in Deep Structure as verbs and those which are represented as nouns is essentially the amount of difference or change we experience in what is represented: *chairs* change slowly and undramatically, while *meetings* change more quickly and dramatically.

5. We will return to consider this subject systematically in Chapter 6 under the title of *Reference Structures* — the sum total of the client's experience — the source from which the full linguistic representation is derived.

6. The limiting case is the physical therapies (e.g., Rolfing, Bioenergetics, Shiatsu, ...) which emphasize working on the physical representational system — that is, human beings represent their experiences in their body posture, movements, typical muscle contractions, tonus.... We return to this topic in Chapter 6. Even in this limiting case, the therapist and the client, typically, talk to one another.

7. This is the focus of Chapter 6 and of *Structure of Magic II.*

8. In fact, from the discussion of the types of deletion transformations in Chapter 2, it follows that every case of Free Deletion is the deletion of a Deep Structure noun argument which had no referential index.

9. The intentional-extensional distinction is borrowed from logic. An extensional definition of a set is one which specifies what the members of the set are by simply listing (i.e., enumerating) them; an intentional definition of a set is one which specifies what the members of the set are by giving a rule or procedure which sorts the world into members and non-members of the set. For example, the set of all humans over six feet in height who live in Ozona, Texas, can be given extentially by a list of the people who, in fact, live in Ozona, Texas, and are taller than six feet, or intentionally by a procedure, say, for example:

(a) Go to the official directory of residents of Ozona, Texas.

(b) Find each person on the list and determine whether he is taller than two yardsticks placed end to end.

Korzybski (1933, Chap. 1) has an interesting discussion of this distinction. Notice that, in general, lists or a set specified extentionally have referential indices while sets intentionally given have no referential index.

10. We say *necessarily* as models are, by definition, reduced with respect to what they represent. This reduction is at the same time their value and their danger, as we discussed in Chapter 1.

11. In listening to and evaluating the Surface Structure answers that clients present to these questions, all the Meta-model techniques apply. In addition, we have found it effective to demand that the clients give *how* (i.e., process) answers rather than *why* (i.e., justification) answers to these questions.

Chapter 4

INCANTATIONS FOR GROWTH AND POTENTIAL

In the last chapter, we presented the Meta-model for therapy. This Meta-model is based on the intuitions which you already have available to you as native speakers of your language. The terminology, however, that we have adapted from linguistics may be new to you. This chapter is designed to present material which allows you to familiarize yourself with how to apply, specifically, the Meta-model. We recognize that, just as with any new set of tools, making ourselves competent with it requires some initially focused attention. This chapter provides each therapist who wishes to incorporate this Meta-model into his techniques and way of proceeding in the therapeutic encounter an opportunity to work with the principles and materials of the Meta-model. By doing this, you will be able to sensitize yourself, to be able to hear the structure of the verbal communications in the therapeutic encounter, and, thereby, to sharpen your intuitions.

The various specific linguistic phenomena which we will present that you will come to recognize and act upon are the specific ways the three universals of human modeling are realized in human language systems. As we introduce each specific linguistic phenomenon, we will identify which of these processes — Generalization, Deletion, or Distortion — is involved. The point is for you to come to recognize and obtain from the client communication which consists wholly of sentences which are well formed in therapy. You, as a native speaker, are able to determine which sentences are well formed in English; the following examples are designed to sharpen your ability to detect what is well formed in therapy — a subset of sentences that are well formed in English. We will present the material in two steps: recognition of what is well formed in therapy and what to do when you have identified in therapy a sentence which is not well formed.

EXERCISE A

One of the most useful skills that you can exercise as a therapist is that of distinguishing what clients represent with their Surface Structures from what you may understand their surface to imply. The question of therapists projecting onto their clients is not a new one. Also, even if a therapist may from his experience understand more about what a client is saying than the client himself may realize, the ability to distinguish is vital. If the client fails to represent something the therapist understands to be there, it is just that piece of information the client may have left out of his representation, or it's just that piece of information which may cue the therapist to use some technique of intervention. In any event, the ability to distinguish what is represented from what you, yourself, supply is vital.

The difference between what you, as a therapist, may understand the client's Surface Structure to imply and what that Surface Structure literally represents comes from you. Those elements that you, yourself, supply may or may not fit the client's model. There are a number of ways to determine whether what you supply is fitting for the client. Your skill as a therapist will increase as your skill in making this distinction increases. What we would like you to do next is to read the following sentence, then close your eyes and form a visual image of what the sentence represents.

The client: *I'm afraid!*

Now examine your image. It will include some visual representation of the client and some representation of the client's being afraid. Any detail beyond these two images was supplied by you. For instance, if you supplied any representation of what the client fears, it came from you and may or may not be accurate. Try this once and read this second Surface Structure; close your eyes and make a visual image.

The client: *Mary hurt me.*

Now examine your image. It will include some visual representation of some person (Mary) and some visual representation of the client. Now look closely at how you represented the process of hurting. The verb hurting is a very vague and unspecific word. If you represented the process of hurting, study your image carefully. Perhaps you had an image of Mary physically striking the client, or perhaps an image of Mary saying something mean to the client. You may have had an image of Mary walking through the room that the client was sitting in without speaking to the client. All of these are possible representations of the client's Surface Structure. In each of them you have added something to the representation of the verb to form an image for yourself. You have ways of determining which, if any, of these representations fits the client — you may ask the client to more fully specify the verb *hurt*, ask the client to enact a specific situation in which Mary hurt him, etc. The important piece is your ability to distinguish between what you supply and what the client is representing with his Surface Structure.

DELETION

The purpose of recognizing deletions is to assist the client in restoring a fuller representation of his experiences. Deletion is a process which removes portions of the original experience (the world) or full linguistic representation (Deep Structure). The linguistic process of deletion is a transformational process — the result of deletion transformations — and a special case of the general modeling phenomenon of Deletion wherein the model we create is reduced with respect to the thing being modeled. Deep Structure is the full linguistic representation. The representation of this representation is the Surface Structure — the actual sentence that the client says to communicate his full linguistic model or Deep Structure. As native speakers of English, therapists have intuitions which allow them to determine whether the Surface Structure represents the full Deep Structure or not. Thus, by comparing the Surface Structure and the Deep Structure, the therapist can determine what is missing. Example:

(1) *I'm confused.*

The basic process word is the verb *confuse*. The verb *confuse* has the potential of occurring in sentences with two arguments or noun phrases — in sentences such as:

(2) *I'm confused by people.*

Since the verb *confuse* occurs in sentence (2) with two argument nouns (*I* and *people*), the therapist can conclude that Surface Structure (1) is not a full representation of the Deep Structure from which it was derived. In a step-by-step format, the procedure can be outlined as follows:

>   Step 1: *Listen* to the Surface Structure the client presents;
>   Step 2: Identify the verbs in that Surface Structure;
>   Step 3: Determine whether the verbs can occur in a sentence which is fuller — that is, has more arguments or noun phrases in it than the original.

If the second sentence has more argument nouns than the original Surface Structure presented by the client, the original Surface Structure is incomplete — a portion of the Deep Structure has been deleted. The first step in learning to recognize deletions is to identify sentences in which deletions have occurred. Thus, for example, sentence (3) is an essentially complete representation of its Deep Structure:

(3) *George broke the chair.*

On the other hand, sentence (4) is an incomplete representation of its Deep Structure:

(4) *The chair was broken.*

The following set of sentences contains some Surface Structures which are complete — no deletions — and some which are incomplete — deletions have occurred. Your task is to identify which of the following set of Surface Structures are complete and which contain deletions. Remember that you decide whether deletions have occurred — some of the sentences may be ill formed in therapy for reasons other than deletion. Additional exercises will give you practice in correcting the other things about these sentences which make them ill formed in therapy.

(5) *I feel happy.*   incomplete
(6) *I'm interested in continuing this.*   complete
(7) *My father was angry.*   incomplete
(8) *This exercise is boring.*   incomplete
(9) *I'm irritated about that.*   complete

The set of sentences below consists wholly of Surface Structures which are incomplete. For each one, you are to find another sentence which has the same process word or verb and which is fuller — that is, has more noun phrases or arguments. Next to each of the incomplete sentences, we have provided an example of a fuller version using the same verb. We suggest that you cover the fuller version, which we have provided, with paper and write out a fuller version of your own before looking at the one we present.

For example, with the Surface Structure:

    (10) *I'm scared.*

one fuller version would be:

    (11) *I'm scared of people.*

or another would be the Surface Structure:

    (12) *I'm scared of spiders.*

The point, of course, is not to try to guess which fuller version we would happen to present, but to provide yourself with the experience of finding fuller versions of incomplete Surface Structures.

(13) *I have a problem.*	I have a problem with people.
(14) *You're excited.*	You're excited about being here.
(15) *I'm sad.*	I'm sad about my mother.
(16) *I'm fed up.*	I'm fed up with you.
(17) *You're disturbing.*	You're disturbing me.

The next group of sentences consists of Surface Structures which have more than one verb and may have zero, one or two deletions. Your task is to determine whether deletions have occurred and, if so, how many. Remember to check each verb separately as each may be independently associated with deletions.

    For example, the Surface Structure

    (18) *I don't know what to say.*

has one deletion associated with the verb *say* (say to whom).

    The Surface Structure

    (19) *I said that I would try.*

has two deletions, one associated with the verb *said* (said to whom) and one with the verb *try* (try what).

(20) *I talked to a man who was bored.*	2 deletions: 1 with *talked*, 1 with *bored*.
(21) *I hoped to see my parents.*	no deletion
(22) *I want to hear.*	1 deletion: with *hear*.
(23) *My husband claimed he was frightened.*	2 deletions: 1 with *claimed*, 1 with *frightened*.
(24) *I laughed and then I left home.*	1 deletion: with *laughed*.

In each of the following Surface Structures, there is at least one deletion. Find a fuller version for each Surface Structure.

(25) *You always talk as though you're mad.*

You always talk *to me* as though you're mad *at someone.*

(26) *My brother swears that my parents can't cope.*

My brother swears *to me* that my parents can't cope *with him.*

(27) *Everybody knows that you can't win.*

Everybody knows that you can't win *what you need.*

(28) *Communicating is hard for me.*

My communicating *to you my hopes about changing myself* is hard for me.

(29) *Running away doesn't help.*

My running away *from my home* doesn't help *me.*

One of the ways in which Deep Structure process words may occur in Surface Structure is in the form of an adjective which modifies a noun. In order for this to happen, deletions must occur. For example, the Surface Structure
(30) *I don't like unclear people.*
contains the adjective *unclear.* Another Surface Structure which is closely associated with this last sentence is[1]
(31) *I don't like people who are unclear.*
In both of these Surface Structures, there have been deletions associated with the word *unclear* (*unclear to whom about what*). Thus, one fuller version is:
(32) *I don't like people who are unclear to me about what they want.*
In the next group of Surface Structures, identify the deletions and present a fuller version of each of the sentences.

(33) *I laughed at the irritating man.*	I laughed at the man who irritated *me.*
(34) *You always present stupid examples.*	You always present examples *to me* which are stupid *to me.*
(35) *Self-righteous people burn me up.*	People who are self-righteous *about drugs* burn me up.
(36) *The unhappy letter surprised me.*	The letter which made *me* unhappy surprised me.
(37) *The overwhelming price of food disturbs me.*	The price of food which overwhelms *me* disturbs me.

The point of practicing recognition of deletions in Surface Structures is to make you conscious of and to sharpen the intuitions that you already have as a native speaker. The point is to be aware that deletions have occurred. The next section is designed to allow you to practice assisting the client in recovering the deleted material.

WHAT TO DO

Once the therapist has recognized that the Surface Structure the client has presented is incomplete, the next task is to help the client recover the deleted material. The most direct approach we are aware of is to ask specifically for what is missing. For example, the client says:

(38) *I'm upset.*

The therapist recognizes that the Surface Structure is an incomplete representation of the Deep Structure from which it came. Specifically, it is a reduced version of a Deep Structure which has a fuller Surface Structure representation of the form:

(39) *I'm upset about someone/something.*
Thus, to recover the missing material, the therapist asks:

(40) *Whom/what are you upset about?*
or more simply

(41) *about whom/what?*

In the following group of Surface Structures, your task is to formulate the question or questions which most directly ask for the deleted material. We've provided examples of the kinds of questions which will elicit the deleted material. Again, we suggest that you cover the questions which we have provided and work out your own appropriate questions for each of the incomplete Surface Structures.

(42) *I feel happy.*	happy about whom/what?
(43) *My father was angry.*	angry at whom/what?
(44) *This exercise is boring.*	boring to whom?
(45) *I'm scared.*	scared of whom/what?
(46) *I have a problem.*	a problem with whom/what?
(47) *I don't know what to do.*	to do about whom/what?
(48) *I said that I would try.*	said to whom? try what?
(49) *I talked to a man who was bored.*	talked about what? bored with whom/what?
(50) *I want to hear.*	want to hear whom/what?
(51) *My husband claimed he was frightened.*	claimed to whom? frightened about whom/what?

(52) *You always talk as though you're mad.*   talk to whom? mad at whom/what?

(53) *My brother swears that. my parents can't cope.*   swears to whom? can't cope with whom/what?

(54) *Communicating is hard for me.*   whose communicating? communicating about what? to whom?

(55) *Running away doesn't help.*   whose running away? running away from whom/what?

(56) *I don't like unclear people.*   unclear about what? unclear to whom?

(57) *I laughed at the irritating man.*   the man who was irritating to whom?

(58) *You always present stupid examples.*   present examples to whom? examples who thinks are stupid?

(59) *Self-righteous people burn me up.*   self-righteous about what?

(60) *The unhappy letter surprised me.*   whom did the letter make unhappy?

(61) *The overwhelming price of food disturbs me.*   who was overwhelmed?

SOME SPECIAL CASES OF DELETION

We have identified three special classes of Deletions. These are special in the sense that we encounter them frequently in therapy, and the Surface Structure forms that they have can be identified directly.

Class I: Real Compared to What?

The first special class of deletions which we wish to identify involves comparatives and superlatives. Specifically, the portion of the Deep Structure deleted is one of the terms of a comparative or superlative construction. Comparatives and superlatives have two forms in English.

(A) Adjective, plus the ending *er*

        as in: fast*er*

                bett*er*

                smart*er*

and Adjective plus the ending *est*

        as in: fast*est*

                b*est*

                smart*est*

              or

(B) *more/less* plus Adjective

        as in: *more* interesting

                more important

                less intelligent

and *most/least* plus Adjective

        as in: *most* interesting

                most important

                least intelligent

Comparatives, as the name suggests, involve a comparison of (minimally) two distinct things. For example, the Surface Structure:

(62) *She is better for me than my mother.*

includes both of the things compared (*she* and *my mother*). The class of Surface Structure which we characterize as involving the deletion of one term of the comparative construction includes, for example:

(63) *She is better for me.*

where one term of the comparison has been deleted. This kind of deletion is also present in Surface Structures such as:

(64) *She is a better woman for me.*

where the comparative adjective appears in front of the noun to which it applies.

The comparatives formed with *more* appear in the two examples:

(65) *She is more interesting to me.*

(66) *She is a more interesting woman to me.*

Again, one of the terms of the comparative has been deleted. In the case of superlatives, one member of some set is selected and identified as most characteristic or having the highest value in the set. For example, in the Surface Structure:

(67) *She is the best.*

(68) *She is the most interesting.*

the set from which *she* has been selected is not mentioned.

The following set of Surface Structures is composed of examples of deletion of one term of a comparative or the deletion of the reference set or a superlative. These examples are presented to allow you to develop your ability to identify deletions of this class.

(69) *She is most difficult.*

(70) *He chose the best.*

(71) *That is the least difficult.*

(72) *She always leaves the harder job for me.*

(73) *I resent happier people.*

(74) *More aggressive men get what they want.*

(75) *The best answer is always more difficult to find.*

(76) *I've never seen a funnier man.*

In coping with this class of deletions, the therapist will be able to recover the deleted material using two simple questions:

For comparatives:

The comparative adjective, plus compared to what? e.g., more aggressive compared to what? or, funnier than what?

For superlatives:

The superlative, plus with respect to what? e.g., the best answer with respect to what? the most difficult with respect to what?

In a step-by-step format, the procedure is:

Step 1: *Listen* to the client, examining the client's Surface Structure for the grammatical markers of the comparative and superlative construction; i.e., Adjective plus *er, more/less* plus Adjective, Adjective plus *est, most/least* plus Adjective.

Step 2: In the case of comparatives occurring in the client's Surface Structuring, determine whether both terms that are being compared are present; in the case of superlatives, determine whether the reference set is present.

Step 3: For each deleted portion, recover the missing material by using the questions suggested above.

Class II: Clearly and Obviously

The second class of special deletions can be identified by *ly* adverbs occurring in the Surface Structures the client presents. For example, the client says:

(77) *Obviously, my parents dislike me.*

or

(78) *My parents obviously dislike me.*

Notice that these Surface Structures can be paraphrased by the sentence

(79) *It is obvious that my parents dislike me.*

Once this form is available, the therapist can more easily identify what portion of the Deep Structure has been deleted. Specifically, in the example, the therapist asks

(80) *To whom is it obvious?*

Surface Structure adverbs which end in *ly* are often the result of deletions of the arguments of a Deep Structure process word or verb. The paraphrase test can be used by the therapist to develop his intuitions in recognizing these adverbs. The test we offer is that, when you encounter an adverb ending with *ly*, attempt to paraphrase the sentence in which it appears by:

(a) Deleting the *ly* from the Surface Structure adverb and placing it in the front of the new Surface Structure you are creating.
(b) Add the phrase *it is* in front of the former adverb.
(c) Ask yourself whether this new Surface Structure means the same thing as the client's original Surface Structure.

If the new sentence is synonymous with the client's original, then the adverb is derived from a Deep Structure verb and deletion is involved. Now, by applying the principles used in recovering missing material to this new Surface Structure, the full Deep Structure representation can be recovered.

In the following set of Surface Structures, determine which of them includes an adverb which has been derived from the Deep Structure verb.

(81) *Unfortunately, you forgot to call me on my birthday.* $=$ It is unfortunate that you forgot to call me on my birthday.

(82) *I quickly left the argument.*	≠	It is quick that I left the argument.
(83) *Surprisingly, my father lied about his drinking.*	=	It is surprising for my father to lie about his drinking.
(84) *She slowly started to cry.*	≠	It is slow that she started to cry.
(85) *They painfully avoided my questions.*	=	It is painful that they avoided my questions.

Once the therapist has identified the adverbs that have been derived from Deep Structure verbs by paraphrasing the client's original Surface Structure, he may apply the methods for recovering deleted material to the Surface Structure paraphrase. In a step-by-step procedure, therapists can handle this particular class of deletion by:

Step 1: *Listen* to the client's Surface Structure for *ly* adverbs.

Step 2: Apply the paraphrase test to each *ly* adverb.

Step 3: If the paraphrase test works, examine the new Surface Structure.

Step 4: Apply the normal methods for recovering the deleted material.

Class III: Modal Operators

The third class of special deletions is particularly important in recovering material which has been deleted in going from the client's experience to his full linguistic representation — Deep Structure. These Surface Structures often involve rules or generalizations that the clients have developed in their models. For example, the client says:

(86) *I have to take other people's feelings into account.*

or

(87) *One must take other people's feelings into account.*

or

(88) *It is necessary to take other people's feelings into account.*

You will be able to identify a number of deletions in each of these Surface Structures on the basis of the principles and exercises we have already presented (e.g., feelings about whom/what?). The deletion we want to draw your attention to here, however, is a larger scale deletion. These Surface Structures make the claim that something must occur — they immediately suggest to us the question, "Or what?" In other words, for us, as therapists, to come to understand the client's model clearly, we must know the consequences to the client of failing to do what the client's Surface Structure claims is necessary. We understand Surface Structures of this class to be of the logical form:

$$\text{It is necessary that } S^1 \text{ or } S^2$$

where S^1 is what the client's Surface Structure claims is necessary and S^2 is what will happen if S^1 isn't done — the consequence or outcome of failing to do S^1 — then S^1 and S^2 are the deleted material. Thus, the therapist may ask:

(89) *Or what will happen?*

or, in a more expanded form

(90) *What would happen if you failed to _____?*

where you substitute the appropriate part of the client's original Surface Structure in the _____. Specifically, using the above as an example, the client says

(91) *One must take other people's feelings into account.*

The therapist may respond,

(92) *Or what will happen?*

or, more fully,[2]

(93) *What would happen if you failed to take other people's feelings into account?*

These Surface Structures can be identified by the presence of what logicians call modal operators of necessity. These have the Surface forms in English of:

have to	as in	*I/You have to . . .*
		one has to . . .
necessary	as in	*It is necessary . . .*
		Necessarily, . . .
should	as in	*One/you/I should . . .*
must	as in	*I/you/one must . . .*

The therapist may use these as cue words to recognize this special class of Surface Structures. In the following set, form a question which asks for the consequence or outcome of failing to do what the Surface Structure claims is necessary. We use the two question forms we suggested above in the following exercise. Note that these are not the only two possible question forms but, in fact, any question which recovers the deleted material is appropriate.

(94) *It is necessary to behave properly in public.*	What would happen if you failed to behave properly in public?
(95) *One should always take people seriously.*	What would happen if you failed to take people seriously?
(96) *I must not get involved too deeply.*	What would happen if you got involved too deeply?
(97) *People have to learn to avoid conflict.*	What would happen if you failed to learn to avoid conflict?

There is a second set of important cue words, what logicians have identified as modal operators of possibility. Again, these operators typically identify rules or generalizations from the client's model. For example, the client says:[3]

(98) *It's not possible to love more than one person at a time.*

or,

(99) *No one can love more than one person at a time.*

or,

(100) *One can't love more than one person at a time.*

or,

(101) *One may not love more than one person at a time.*

or,

(102) *No one is able to love more than one person at a time.*

Again, based on your experience in identifying deletions, you can find in these Surface Structures deletions from the Deep Structure representation. However, we want to identify in these examples a deletion which occurs going from the client's experience to the Deep Structure representation. Specifically, on hearing Surface Structures of this class, we want to ask what it is that makes whatever the client's Surface Structure claims is impossible, impossible. In other words, we understand these Surface Structures to be of the general logical form:

S^1 *prevents* S^2 *from being possible*

where S^2 is what the client's Surface Structure claims is impossible and S^1 is the missing material. Thus, the therapist may ask,

(103) *What makes*_____*impossible?*

or,

(104) *What prevents you from*_____*?*

or,

(105) *What blocks you from*_____*?*

or,

(106) *What stops you from*_____*?*

where the_____contains what the client's Surface Structure claims is impossible.

Specifically, using the above example, the therapist may ask,

(107) *What makes your loving more than one person impossible?*

or,

(108) *What prevents you from loving more than one person at a time?*

or,

(109) *What blocks you from loving more than one person at a time?*

or,

(110) *What stops you from loving more than one person at a time?*

Surface Structures of this class can be easily identifed by the following cue words and phrases:

not possible	as in	*it's not possible*
can	as in	*no one can* *nobody can*
may	as in	*no one may* *nobody may*
can't	as in	*I/you/one/people can't*
able	as in	*no one is able* *nobody is able*
impossible	as in	*it's impossible*
unable	as in	*I/you/one/people are unable*

These cue words occurring in the client's Surface Structures identify rules or generalizations which correspond to limits in the client's model of the world. Such limits are often associated with the client's experience of limited choice or an unsatisfactory, limited set of options. In the following set of Surface Structures, form a question for each which (when answered) would recover the deleted material.

(111)	*It's impossible to find someone who's really sensitive.*	What prevents you from finding someone who's really sensitive?
(112)	*I can't understand my wife.*	What prevents you from understanding your wife?
(113)	*I am unable to express myself.*	What prevents you from expressing yourself?
(114)	*No one is able to understand me.*	What prevents them from understanding you?

The value of identifying and recovering deletions of this scope can hardly be overestimated, as they directly involve portions of the client's model wherein he experiences limited options or choices. In a step-by-step outline:

Step 1: *Listen* to the client; examine the client's Surface Structure for the presence of the cue words and phrases identified in this section.

Step 2: (a) If modal operators of necessity are present, use a question form asking for the deleted consequence or outcome of failing to do what the client's Surface Structure claims is necessary, and (b) if the modal operators of possibility are present, use a question form asking for the deleted material which makes impossible what the client's Surface Structure claims is impossible.

DISTORTION — NOMINALIZATIONS

The linguistic process of nominalization is one way the general modeling process of Distortion occurs in natural language systems. The purpose of recognizing nominalizations is to assist the client in re-connecting his linguistic model with the ongoing dynamic processes of life. Specifically, reversing nominalizations assists the client in coming to see that what he had considered an event, finished and beyond his control, is an ongoing process which can be changed. The linguistic process of nominalization is a complex transformational process whereby a process word or verb in the Deep Structure appears as an event word, or noun, in the Surface Structure. The first step in reversing nominalizations is to recognize them. Therapists, as native speakers, may use their intuitions to identify which elements of the Surface Structure are, in fact, nominalizations. For example, in the Surface Structure,

(115) *I regret my decision to return home.*

the event word or noun *decision* is a nominalization. This means that in the Deep Structure representation there appeared a process word or verb, in this case the verb *decide*.

(116) *I regret that I'm deciding to return home.*

True nouns will not fit into the blank in the phrase *an ongoing _____*, in a well-formed way. For example, the true nouns *chair, kite, lamp, fern*, etc., do not fit in a well-formed way — **an ongoing chair, *an ongoing kite*, etc. However, nouns such as *decision, marriage, failure*, derived from Deep Structure verbs, do fit — *an ongoing decision, an ongoing marriage*, etc. Thus, therapists may train their intuitions using this simple test. In a step-by-step format, the therapist may recognize nominalizations by:

Step 1: *Listen* to the Surface Structure presented by the client.

Step 2: For each of the elements of the Surface Structure which is not a process word or verb, ask yourself whether it describes some event which is actually a process in the world, or ask yourself whether there is some verb which sounds/looks like it and is close to it in meaning.

Step 3: Test to see whether the event word fits into the blank in the syntactic frame, *an ongoing_____*.

For each non-verb occurring in the client's Surface Structure which either describes an event which you can associate with a process or for which you can find a verb which is close in sound/appearance and meaning, a nominalization has occurred. For example, there are several nominalizations in the sentence:

(117) *Their failure to see their own children received no recognition.*

Both event words *failure* and *recognition* are derived from Deep Structure verbs *(an ongoing failure, an ongoing recognition)*. The Surface Structure

(118) *I dashed in front of the car.*

on the other hand, contains no nominalizations.

In the following set of Surface Structures, you are simply to decide which sentences contain nominalizations. Again, we suggest you judge each Surface Structure for yourself before looking at the comments we have provided.

(119) *My divorce is painful.*   1 nominalization *(divorce)*

(120) *Our terror is blocking us.*   1   "   *(terror)*

(121) *My wife's laughter causes my anger.*   2   "   *(laughter, anger)*

(122) *Your refusal to leave here forces my departure.*   2   "   *(refusal, departure)*

(123) *Your perceptions are seriously wrong.*   1   "   *(perception)*

(124) *Your projection causes me injury.*   2   "   *(projection, injury)*

(125) *My confusion has a tendency to give me no relief.*   3   "   *(confusion, tendency, relief)*

(126) *I resent your question.*   1   "   *(question)*

(127) *I'm afraid of*   2 nominalization *(rage,*
      both your rage   *help)*
      and your help.

(128) *His intuitions*   1   "   *(intuitions)*
      are remarkable.

In the next set of Surface Structures, reverse each nominalization by creating a closely associated Surface Structure which translates the nominalization back into an ongoing process. For example, from the sentence

(129) *I am surprised at her*   ⟶   I am surprised that she
       resistance to me.   is resisting me.

The point here is not whether you can create a new sentence which matches the one we suggest, but that you sharpen your ability to translate a nominalized process back into an ongoing process. The sentences we offer are only examples. Remember that neither the original Surface Structure nor the ones corrected for nominalization will be well formed in therapy until they meet all the other well-formedness conditions.

My divorce is painful.	My wife and I divorcing is painful.
Our terror is blocking us.	Our being terrified is blocking us.
My wife's laughter causes my anger.	My wife's laughing causes me to feel angry.
Your refusal to leave here forces my departure.	Your refusing to leave here forces me to depart.
Your perceptions are seriously wrong.	The way you are/What you are perceiving is seriously wrong.

Your projection causes me injury.	The way that you are/What you are projecting injures me.
My confusion has a tendency to give me no relief.	My being confused tends to stop me from feeling relieved.
I resent your question.	I resent what you are asking/the way you are asking me.
I'm afraid of both your rage and your help.	I'm afraid of both the way you rage at me and the way you help me.
His intuitions are remarkable.	The way he intuites things/What he intuites is remarkable.

We are aware that we have a number of choices when we encounter nominalizations. We may choose to question the nominalization directly. For example, given the Surface Structure:

(130) *The decision to return home bothers me.*

we may directly challenge the idea that *the decision* is an irrevocable, fixed and finished event from which the client has disassociated himself by asking,

(131) *Is there any way that you can imagine changing your decision?*

or, again,

(132) *What is it that prevents you from changing your decision?*

or, again,

(133) *What would happen if you reconsidered and decided not to return home?*

In each of these cases, the therapist's questions require a response by the client which involves his taking some responsibility for the process of deciding. In any event, the therapist's questioning helps the client to re-connect his linguistic model of the world with the ongoing processes which are present there.

Nominalizations are complex psychologically as well as linguistically. Our experience is that they rarely occur by themselves; rather, we encounter them more frequently in a form which involves violations of one or more of the other well-formed-in-therapy conditions. Since we have already presented the exercises on deletion, we will now give you a set of Surface Structures which contain both nominalizations and deletions. We ask that you identify both the nominalization and the deletion, and that you formulate a question or series of questions which both translates the nominalization back into a process form and asks for the material which has been deleted. For example, given the Surface Structure

The decision to return home bothers me.

one question which both translates the nominalization back into a process form and simultaneously asks for the deleted material is:

(134) *Who is deciding to return home?*

Again, we suggest that you attempt to formulate your own question(s) before looking at the examples we offer. The example questions we present are dense — we suggest in practice that a series of questions be used, asking for a piece at a time.

(135) *My pain is overwhelming.*

Your feeling pain about whom/what is overwhelming whom?

(136) *It's my fear that gets in my way.*

Your being afraid of whom/what gets in your way of what?

(137) *I have hope.*

What are you hoping for?

(138) *My son's beliefs worry me.*

Your son believes what that worries you?

(139) *Your bigoted suspicion an-
noys me.*

Bigoted toward
whom/what?
What is it that
you are
suspecting?

EXERCISE B

Since in Meta-model training seminars we have found nominalizations to be the most difficult phenomena for people to learn to
recognize, we have devised the following exercise.

Form a visual image from the following sentences. In
each case, see if you can imagine placing each of the
non-process or non-verb words in a wheelbarrow.

I want to make a chair.
I want to make a decision.

Notice that all the non-verb words in the first sentence *(I,
chair)* can be placed in your mental wheelbarrow. This is
not the case with the second sentence *(I, decision). I* can
be placed in a wheelbarrow but a *decision* cannot. In the
following sets of sentences, use this same visual test to
train yourself in recognizing nominalizations.

I have a lot of *frustration.*
I have a lot of *green marbles.*

I expect a *letter.*
I expect *help.*

My *fear* is just too big.
My *coat* is just too big.

I lost my *book.*
I lost my *temper.*

I need *water.*
I need *love.*

Horses frighten *me.*
Failure frightens *me.*

The *tension* bothers *me.*
The *dragon* bothers *me.*

At least one nominalization occurs in each of the preceding pairs. You may check the accuracy of your visual test by now applying the purely linguistic test, *an ongoing* in front of the nominalization. The same word which fits into the linguistic frame — *an ongoing* _____ — will not fit into your mental wheelbarrow.

GENERALIZATION

How To Get a Clear Image of the Client's Model

One of the universal processes which occur when humans create models of their experiences is that of Generalization. Generalization may impoverish the client's model by causing loss of the detail and richness of their original experiences. Thus, generalization prevents them from making distinctions which would give them a fuller set of choices in coping with any particular situation. At the same time, the generalization expands the specific painful experience to the level of being persecuted by the universe (an insurmountable obstacle to coping). For example, the specific painful experience "Lois doesn't like me" generalizes to "Women don't like me." The purpose of challenging the client's generalizations is to:

(1) Re-connect the client's model with his experience.
(2) Reduce the insurmountable obstacles which result from generalizations to something definite with which he can begin to cope.
(3) Insure detail and richness are present in the client's model, thus creating choices based on distinctions which were not previously available.

Linguistically, we are aware of two important ways which we use to identify the generalizations in the client's model. At the same time, these provide us with a vehicle for challenging these generalizations. These are the processes of:

(1) Checking for referential indices for nouns and event words;
(2) Checking for fully specified verbs and process words.

Referential Indices

The ability of the therapist to determine whether the Surface Structures presented by the client are connected with the client's experience is essential for successful therapy. One explicit way of determining this is for the therapist to identify words and phrases in the client's Surface Structure which do not have a referential index. For example, in the Surface Structure

(140) *People push me around.*

the noun *people* carries no referential index and, therefore, fails to identify anything specific in the client's experience. On the other hand, the sentence

(141) *My father pushes me around.*

contains two nouns *(my father* and *me),* both bearing a referential index which identifies something specific in the client's model.

Again, a step-by-step procedure is available.

> Step 1: *Listen* to the client's Surface Structure, identifying each non-process word.

> Step 2: For each of these, ask yourself whether it picks out a specific person or thing in the world.

If the word or phrase fails to pick out a specific person or thing, then the therapist has identified a generalization in the client's model. In the following set of Surface Structures, decide for each noun or phrase whether it does or does not have a referential index making it well formed in therapy.

(142) *Nobody pays any attention to what I say.*	*Nobody* and *what* have no referential index.
(143) *I always avoid situations I feel uncomfortable in.*	*Situations I feel uncomfortable in* — no index.
(144) *I like dogs that are friendly.*	*Dogs that are friendly* — no index.
(145) *I saw my mother-in-law yesterday.*	All nouns have indices.
(146) *One should respect others' feelings.*	*One* and *others'* — no indices.
(147) *It's painful for us to see her this way, you know.*	*It, us, you* and *this way* — no indices.
(148) *Let's not get bogged down in details.*	*Us* and *details* — no indices.

> (149) *There's a certain feeling in this room.*   *A certain feeling* — no index.
>
> (150) *Everybody feels that way sometimes.*   *Everybody, that way, sometimes* — no indices.

Once the therapist has identified the words and phrases without referential indices, it is quite easy to ask for these. Only two questions are required:

(151) *Who, specifically?*
(152) *What, specifically?*

In requiring the client to supply referential indices by answering these questions, the client re-connects the generalizations in his model with his experiences. In the next set of Surface Structures, formulate the question appropriate for getting the missing referential index.

> *Nobody pays any attention to what I say.*   Who, specifically? What, specifically, do you say?
>
> *I always avoid situations I feel uncomfortable in.*   What situations, specifically?
>
> *I like dogs that are friendly.*   What dog, specifically?
>
> *It's painful for us to see her this way, you know.*   Who, specifically, is full of pain? Who, specifically, is *us*? What way, specifically? Who, specifically, is *you*?
>
> *Everybody feels that way sometimes.*   Who, specifically? What way, specifically? What time, specifically?

There is a special case which we like to emphasize of certain words which have no referential index. This, specifically, is the set of words which contains universal quantifiers such as *all, each, every, any.* The universal quantifier has a different form when combined with other linguistic elements such as the negative element — *never, nowhere, none, no one, nothing, nobody.* Universal quantifiers, and words and phrases containing them, have no referential index. We use a special form of challenge for the universal quantifier and words and phrases containing it. For example, the Surface Structure presented before:

> *Nobody pays any attention to what I say.*

may be challenged as we suggested before or with the challenge:

> (153) *You mean to tell me that NOBODY EVER pays attention to you AT ALL?*

What we are doing here is emphasizing the generalization described by the client's universal quantifier by exaggerating it both by voice quality and by inserting additional universal quantifiers in the client's original Surface Structure. This challenge identifies and emphasizes a generalization in the client's model. At the same time, this form of challenge asks clients if there are any exceptions to their generalizations. A single exception to the generalization starts the client on the process of assigning referential indices and insures the detail and richness in the client's model necessary to have a variety of options for coping.

> **C:** *Nobody pays any attention to what I say.*
> **T:** *Do you mean to tell me that NOBODY EVER pays attention to you AT ALL?*
> **C:** *Well, not exactly.*
> **T:** *OK, then; who, specifically, doesn't pay attention to you?*

Once the therapist has identified a generalization it can be challenged in several ways.

(a) As mentioned in the section on universal quantifiers, generalizations can be challenged by emphasizing the universal nature of the claim by the Surface Structure by inserting universal quantifiers into that Surface Structure. The therapist now asks the client to check the new generalization explicit in this Surface Structure against his experience. For example, the client says:

> **C:** *It's impossible to trust anyone.*
> **T:** *It's always impossible for anyone to trust anyone?*

The purpose of the therapist's challenge to the generalization is to re-connect the client's generalization with the client's experience. The therapist has other options in the way that he may challenge the client's generalizations.

(b) Since the purpose of challenging the client's generalizations is to re-connect the client's representation with his experience, one very direct challenge is, literally, to ask the client whether he has had an experience which contradicts his own generalization. For example, the client says:

    C: *It's impossible to trust anyone.*

    T: *Have you ever had the experience of trusting someone?*

or

    Have you ever trusted anyone?

Notice that, linguistically, the therapist is doing several things: Relativizing the generalization to the client's experience by shifting the referential index from no index (the missing indirect object of the predicate *impossible* [i.e., *impossible for whom?*] and the missing subject of the verb *trust*) to linguistic forms carrying the client's referential index (i.e., *you*).

(c) A third way of challenging generalizations of this form is to ask the client whether he can imagine an experience which would contradict the generalization. The client says:

    C: *It's impossible to trust anyone.*

    T: *Can you imagine any circumstance in which you could trust someone?*

or,

    Can you fantasize a situation in which you could trust someone?

Once the client has succeeded in imagining or fantasizing a situation which contradicts the generalization, the therapist may assist the client in opening up this part of his model by asking what the difference between the client's experience and the client's fantasy is, or what prevents the client from achieving the fantasy. Notice that one of the most powerful techniques here is to connect the client with the immediate experience that he is having, i.e., relativize the generalization to the process of ongoing therapy directly. The therapist may respond:

    Do you trust me right now in this situation?

If the client responds positively, his generalization has been contradicted. If he responds negatively, all the other techniques are available, e.g., asking what, specifically, is preventing the client from trusting the therapist in this situation.

(d) In the event the client is unable to fantasize an experience which contradicts his generalization, the therapist may choose to search his own models to find a case in which he has had an experience which contradicts the client's generalization. If the therapist can find some experience of his own which is common enough that the client also may have had it, he may ask whether that experience contradicts the client's generalization.

    C: *It's impossible to trust anyone.*

T: *Have you ever gone to the doctor (or to the dentist, ridden in a bus or taxi or airplane, or . . .)? Did you trust the doctor (or dentist, or bus driver, or . . .)?*

Once the client has admitted that he has had an experience which contradicts his generalization, he has re-connected his representation with his experience and the therapist is able to explore the differences with him.

(e) Another approach to challenging the client's generalization is for the therapist to determine what makes the generalization possible or impossible. This technique is described in the section on modal operators of necessity (this chapter, p. 69).

C: *It's impossible to trust anyone.*

T: *What stops you from trusting anyone?*

or,

What would happen if you trusted someone?

(f) Often the client will offer generalizations from his model in the form of generalizations about another person. For example:

C: *My husband is always arguing with me.*

or,

My husband never smiles at me.

Notice that the predicates *argue with* and *smile at* describe processes which are occurring between two people. The form of the two sentences is: The subject (the active agent), the verb (the name of the process), and the object (the non-active person involved in the process). In both of the above examples, the client represents himself as the passive member of the process — the object of the predicate — thus avoiding any responsibility for the process or relationship. The generalizations which are reported by the client in these two Surface Structures involved a special kind of deletion — the Deep Structure is adequately represented by these Surface Structures but there is a deletion in the process of representing the client's experience by these Deep Structures. In other words, the client has deleted a portion of his experience when he represented it with the Deep Structure from which these Surface Structures are derived. The image of the processes or relationships of *arguing with* and *smiling at* are incomplete as only one person in the relationship is being described as having an active role. When faced with Surface Structures of this type, the therapist has the choice of asking for the way the person characterized as passive is involved in the process. One very specific and often potent way of asking for this information is to shift the referential indices contained in the client's generalization. In the examples given the shift would be:[4] (See page 86)

Making these shifts in referential indices, the therapist creates a

| *My husband*   **and** | *me*
| *me (the client)* | *My husband*

new Surface Structure based on the client's original Surface Structure. Specifically:

| *My husband always argues with me.*
| *I always argue with my husband,*

and

| *My husband never smiles at me.*
| *I never smile at my husband.*

Once the referential indices shift, the therapist may then ask the client to verify these new Surface Structures with the question:

Do you always argue with your husband?

and

Do you ever smile at your husband?

Here an additional linguistic distinction is available which may be useful to the therapist: predicates which describe processes or relationships between two people are of two different logical types:

(a) **Symmetrical predicates:** Predicates which, if accurate, necessarily imply that their converse is also accurate. The predicate *argue with* is of this logical type. If the Surface Structure:

My husband always argues with me.

is accurate, then necessarily the Surface Structure:

I always argue with my husband.

is also accurate. This property of symmetrical predicates is represented linguistically by the general form:

If a Surface Structure of the form *X Predicate Y* is true and Predicate is a symmetrical predicate, then necessarily the Surface Structure of the form *Y Predicate X* is also true.

If you are arguing with me, then, necessarily, I am arguing with you. This same point is made by the expression, "It takes two to make an argument." In the case of applying the referential index shift technique to Surface Structures the therapist knows that the result will be a generalization which is necessarily implied by the original. This technique assists the client in re-connecting his representation with his experience.

(b) **Non-Symmetrical Predicates:** Predicates which describe a relationship whose converse is not necessarily true. The predicate

smile at is of this logical type. If the Surface Structure:
> *My husband never smiles at me.*

is accurate, then it may or may not be true that the converse Surface Structure (with the referential indices shifted) is also accurate:
> *I never smile at my husband.*

While there is no logical necessity that the converse of a Surface Structure with a non-symmetrical predicate will be accurate, our experience has been that the converse is frequently psychologically accurate. That is, often when the client states a generalization about another person (especially if the relationship between the client and the person being characterized is an important one for the client), the converse is true. Traditionally, this phenomenon has been referred to in some forms of psychotherapy as projection. Whether the converse of the client's Surface Structure turns out to be accurate, by asking the client to verify it, the therapist begins to recover the missing material and to help the client re-connect his representation with his experience.

    (c) Clients sometimes present generalizations from their model in the form:
> *X or Y*

For example, a client says:
> **C:** *I have to take care of other people.*

to which the therapist may reply (as outlined in the section on modal operators):
> **T:** *Or what will happen?*
> **C:** *Or they won't like me.*

Thus, the full generalization is:
> *I have to take care of other people or they won't like me.*

This generalization involves a claim that there is a necessary causal relationship between the client's taking care of (or not taking care of) other people and other people's liking the client. The same claim is involved in the Surface Structure:
> *If I don't take care of people, they won't like me.*

In fact, within formal systems, the logical equivalence holds.[5]

$$X \text{ or } Y \quad \equiv \quad \text{not } X \longrightarrow Y$$

Whether the clients present their generalizations in the *X or Y* form spontaneously or supply the second portion — the outcome or consequence — upon questioning, their generalizations may be restated by the therapist in the equivalent *If . . . then . . .* form. Once the therapist has had the client verify the *If . . . then . . .* form of his generalization, he may challenge it by introducing negatives into both portions of the generalization and presenting the resulting Surface Structure to the client:

If you do take care of other people, they will like you?

The therapist may use this reversal technique in combination with other techniques; for example, some of those discussed under modal operators or universal quantifiers, yielding the Surface Structure challenge:

$$\textit{If you do take care of other people, will they} \begin{Bmatrix} \text{necessarily} \\ \text{always} \end{Bmatrix} \textit{like you?}$$

Complex Generalization — Equivalence

We want to point out one additional, frequently occurring form of generalization which is somewhat more complex than the ones which we have so far considered in this section. These complex generalizations involve Surface Structures which are equivalent in the client's model. Typically, the client says one of these Surface Structures, pauses, and then says the second. The two Surface Structures characteristically have the same syntactic form. For example, the client says:

My husband never appreciates me. . . . My husband never smiles at me.

The two Surface Structures are syntactically parallel:

$$\text{Noun}^1 - \text{Universal Quantifer} - \text{Verb} - \text{Noun}^2$$

where Noun^1 = my husband

Noun^2 = me (the client)

Notice that one of these Surface Structures (the first) involves a violation of one of the well-formed-in-therapy conditions; specifically, the client is claiming knowledge of one of her husband's inner states *(appreciate)* without stating how she got her knowledge — a case of mind-reading. In the second Surface Structure, the process of one person's smiling or failing to smile at another person is described — a verifiable experience which doesn't require knowledge of the inner state of that other person. Both of these sample Surface Structures are generalizations which may be challenged (using the technique described in the section on universal quantifiers). Here, however, we wish to offer a short-cut technique which often yields dramatic results. The therapist first checks to see if the two Surface Structures are, in fact, equivalents in the client's model. This is easily done by directly asking whether the two Surface Structures are equivalents:

C: *My husband never appreciates me ... My husband never smiles at me.*

T: *Does your husband's not smiling at you always mean that he doesn't appreciate you?*

Here the client is faced with a choice — the client will deny the equivalence and the therapist may ask how the client does, in fact, know that her husband doesn't appreciate her, or the client verifies the equivalence. If the equivalence of these two Surface Structures is verified, the therapist applies the referential index shift technique:

| ↓ *My husband* | | ↓ *me (the client)* |
| ↑ *me (the client)* | | ↑ *My husband* |

This results in the transformation of the Surface Structure from:

> *Does your husband's not smiling at you always mean that he doesn't appreciate you?*

to the Surface Structure:

> *Does your not smiling at your husband always mean that you don't appreciate him?*

Let's review what has happened:

1. The client says two Surface Structures which are separated by a pause and have the same syntactic form — one involving mind-reading, the other not.

2. The therapist checks to see if the two Surface Structures are equivalent.

3. The client verifies their equivalence.

Thus, we have the situation:

> *(X not smiling at Y) = (X doesn't appreciate Y)*
> *where X is the client's husband and Y is the client*

4. The therapist shifts the referential indices and asks the client to verify the new generalization. The new Surface Structure has the same logical form:

> *(X not smiling at Y) = (X doesn't appreciate Y)*
> *where X is the client and Y is the client's husband.*

5. Typically, the client denies the equivalence when she is the active agent subject of the process.

> *(X not smiling at Y) ≠ (X doesn't appreciate Y)*
> *where X is the client and Y is the client's husband*

If the client accepts the new generalization, the therapist has all the usual options for challenging generalization. Our experience is that the client will seldom accept the new generalization.

6. The therapist may now begin to explore the difference between the two situations: the one in which the equivalence holds and the one in which it does not. The client, again, has reconnected her generalization with her experience. The overall exchange looks like:

C: *My husband never appreciates me. . . . My husband never smiles at me.*

T: *Does your husband's not smiling at you always mean that he doesn't appreciate you?*

C: *Yes, that's right!*

T: *Does your not smiling at your husband always mean that you don't appreciate him?*

C: *No, that's not the same thing.*

T: *What's the difference?*

Incompletely Specified Verbs

The second form of generalization which occurs in natural language systems is that of verbs which are not completely specified. For example, in the Surface Structures,

(154) *My mother hurt me.*

(155) *My sister kicked me.*

(156) *My friend touched me on the cheek with her lips.*

the image presented is increasingly more specific and clear. So, in the first, the mother referred to may have caused some physical hurt or the hurt may have been "psychological"; she may have done it with a knife or a word or a gesture, . . . all of this is left incompletely specified. In the next sentence, the sister mentioned may have kicked the speaker with her left or her right foot, but it is specified to have been her foot; where the speaker was kicked is left unspecified. In the third example, the image presented is even more specified — the way the friend mentioned made contact is stated *(touched with her lips)* and the place on the speaker's body where contact was made is also specified *(on the cheek)*. Notice, however, that the duration of the contact, the roughness or gentleness, are left unspecified.[6]

Every verb of which we are aware is incompletely specified to some degree. How clear the image is that the verb presents is determined by two factors:

(1) The meaning of the verb itself. For example, the verb *kiss* is more specific by its meaning alone than the verb *touch* — *kiss* is equivalent to a specific form of touching; namely, *touching with one's lips.*

(2) The amount of information presented by the rest of the sentence in which the verb occurs. For example,

the phrase *hurt by rejecting* is more specified than simply the verb *hurt*.

Since every verb is to some degree incompletely specified, we suggest the following procedure:

Step 1: *Listen* to the client's Surface Structure, identifying the process words or verbs.

Step 2: Ask yourself whether the image presented by the verb in its sentence is clear enough for you to visualize the actual sequence of events being described.

If the therapist finds that the image he has from the verb and the accompanying words and phrases of the client's Surface Structure is not clear enough to visualize the actual sequence of events being described, then he should ask for a more completely specified verb. The question available to the therapist to clarify the poorly focused image is:

How, specifically, did X_____Y?

where X = the subject of the incompletely specified verb and Y = the incompletely specified verb plus the remainder of the client's original Surface Structure.

For example, given the Surface Structure

(157) *Susan hurt me.*

the therapist asks for a more fully specified image with the question

(158) *How, specifically, did Susan hurt you?*

For the next set of Surface Structures, formulate a question which, when answered, would clarify your image of the action being described.

(159) *My children force me to punish them.*

How, specifically, do your children force you to punish them? Also, how, specifically, do you punish your children?

(160) *Sharon is always demanding attention from me.*

How, specifically, does she demand attention from you?

(161) *I always show Jane that I love her.*

How, specifically, do you show Jane that you love her?

(162) *My husband always ig-*   How, specifically, does
     nores me.   your husband ignore
                                   you?

(163) *My family is trying to*   How, specifically, is
     drive me crazy.   your family trying to
                               drive you crazy?

Every Surface Structure which is well formed in English contains a process word or verb. No verbs that we have encountered have been completely specified. Therefore, every one of the client's Surface Structures is the occasion for the therapist to check to see whether the image presented is clear.

PRESUPPOSITIONS

Presuppositions are one linguistic reflex of the process of Distortion. The therapist's purpose in recognizing presuppositions is to assist the client in identifying those basic assumptions which impoverish his model and limit his options in coping. Linguistically, these basic assumptions show up as presuppositions of the client's Surface Structures. For example, to make sense out of the Surface Structure

    (164) *I'm afraid that my son is turning out to be as lazy as*
        my husband.

the therapist has to accept as true the situation expressed by the sentence presupposed by this sentence. Specifically,

    (165) *My husband is lazy.*

Notice that this last Surface Structure, the presupposition of the one before, does not appear directly as any part of the sentence which presupposes it. Linguists have developed a test for determining what the presuppositions of any given sentence are. Adopted for the Meta-model they are

    Step 1: *Listen* for the main process word or verb in the client's Surface Structure — call this Sentence A.

    Step 2: Create a new Surface Structure by introducing the negative word in the client's original Surface Structure on the main verb — call this Sentence B.

    Step 3: Ask yourself what must be true for both A and B to make sense.

All of the things (expressed in the form of other sentences) which must be true for both A and B to make sense are the presuppositions of the client's original sentence. Specifically, in the case of the sentence,

> *I'm afraid that my son is turning out to be as lazy as my husband.*

by introducing the negative on the main verb *(afraid)*, the therapist creates a second sentence,

> (166) *I'm not afraid that my son is turning out to be as lazy as my husband.*

The point here is that, for the therapist to make sense out of this new Surface Structure, it must be true that

> (165) *My husband is lazy.*

Since both the client's original Surface Structure and the new Surface Structure formed from it by introducing the negative element require that this last sentence (165) be true, this last Surface Structure is the presupposition of the client's original sentence.

In the succeeding set of Surface Structures, identify the presuppositions of each of the sentences.

(167) *If you are going to be as unreasonable as you were last time we discussed this, then let's skip it.*	— We discussed something. — You were unreasonable the last time we discussed something.
(168) *If Judy has to be so possessive, then I'd rather not be involved with her.*	Judy is possessive.
(169) *If Fred had enjoyed my company, he wouldn't have left so early.*	Fred didn't enjoy my company.
(170) *If you knew how much I suffered, you wouldn't act this way.*	—I suffer. — You act out this way. — You don't know. . . .
(171) *Since my problem is trivial, I'd rather not take up valuable group time.*	My problem is trivial.

Linguists have identified a large number of specific forms or syntactic environments in language in which presuppositions necessarily occur. For example, any portion of a Surface Structure which occurs after the main verbs *realize, be aware, ignore,* etc., is a presupposition or necessary assumption of that Surface Structure. Notice that these specific forms or syntactic environments are independent of the content or meaning of the words and phrases used. We have included an appendix (Appendix B) which identifies these syntactic environments to assist those who wish to train themselves more thoroughly in the recognition of the language forms which carry presuppositions.

Having identified the presuppositions of the client's Surface Structures, the therapist may now challenge them. Due to the complexity of the presuppositions, the therapist has a number of choices.

1. The therapist may present the client with the presupposition implicit in his original Surface Structure directly. In doing this, the therapist can ask the client to explore this presupposition, using the other well-formed-in-therapy conditions. For example, the client says,

(172) *I'm afraid that my son is turning out to be as lazy as my husband.*

The therapist identifies the presupposition

(173) *My husband is lazy.*

and presents it to the client, asking her how, specifically, her husband is lazy. The client responds with another Surface Structure which the therapist evaluates for well-formedness-in-therapy.

2. The therapist may decide to accept the presupposition and apply the well-formed-in-therapy condition to the client's original Surface Structure, asking to specify the verb, recover the deleted material, etc.

We will present a set of Surface Structures which have presuppositions and give some possible ways of challenging them. Remember that the questions we offer are examples and do not exhaust all the possibilities.

(174) *If my wife is going to be as unreasonable as she was the last time I tried to talk to her about this, then I certainly won't try again.*

What, specifically, seemed unreasonable to you about your wife?
How, specifically, did your wife seem to you to be unreasonable?

(175) *If Judy has to be so possessive, then I'd rather not be involved with her.*   How, specifically, does Judy seem to you to be possessive?

SEMANTIC WELL-FORMEDNESS

The purpose of recognizing sentences which are semantically ill formed is to assist the client in identifying the portions of his model which are distorted in some way that impoverishes the experiences which are available to him. Typically, these impoverishing distortions take the form of limiting the client's options in some way that reduces the client's ability to act. We have identified some frequently occurring classes of semantic ill-formedness which we typically encounter in therapy. We present the linguistic characterization for each class below. The choices which the therapist has for dealing with the first two classes of semantically ill-formed Surface Structures are essentially the same. Therefore, we will present these choices in one section after we have presented both of these classes.

Cause and Effect

This class of semantically ill-formed Surface Structures involves the belief on the part of the speaker that one person (or set of circumstances) may perform some action which necessarily causes some other person to experience some emotion or inner state. Typically, the person experiencing this emotion or inner state is portrayed as having no choice in responding the way he does. For example, the client says,

(176) *My wife makes me feel angry.*

Notice that this Surface Structure presents a vague image in which one human being (identified as *My wife*) performs some action (unspecified) which necessarily causes some other person (identified as *me*) to experience some emotion *(anger)*. Ill-formed Surface Structures which are members of this class can be identified by one of two general forms:

(A) X   Verb   Y   Verb   Adjective
       (cause)   (feel   (some emotion
                          experience)   or
                                          some inner state)

where X and Y are nouns which have different referential

indices, i.e., refer to different people.

The Surface Structure presented above is of this form — namely:

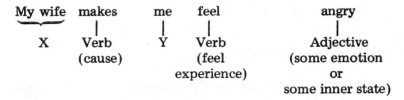

My wife	makes	me	feel	angry
X	Verb (cause)	Y	Verb (feel experience)	Adjective (some emotion or some inner state)

The other general form which we frequently encounter is that of underlying Surface Structures such as:

(177) *Your laughing distracts me.*

The general form is:

(B)   X   Verb   Verb   Y
                                    (cause)

where X and Y are nouns which have different referential indices, i.e., refer to different people.

Applying the general form to the example we have:

Your	laughing	distracts	me
X	Verb	Verb (cause)	Y

We will now present a set of Surface Structures, all of which are semantically ill formed in the way we have been discussing. This is to assist you in training your intuitions to recognize examples of this type of semantic ill-formedness.

(178) *She compels me to be jealous.*

(179) *You always make me feel happy.*

(180) *He forced me to feel bad.*

(181) *She causes me a lot of pain.*

(182) *Your writing on the wall bothers me.*

(183) *Their crying irritates me.*

In addition to Surface Structures which are of these two general forms, there are others which have a different form but have the same meaning relationships. For example, the Surface Structure

(184) *She depresses me.*

carries the same meaning relationship as the Surface Structure

(185) *She makes me feel depressed.*

In fact, to assist therapists in training their intuitions to recognize semantically ill-formed Surface Structures of this type, this paraphrase test can be used. Specifically, if the Surface Structure the client presents can be translated from

| X | Verb | Y |

where X and Y are nouns with different referential indices into the general form (a)

| X | Verb | Y | Verb | Adjective |
| (cause) | | | (feel experience) | (emotion or inner state) |

where the adjective is a form related to the verb in the client's original Surface Structure

and the new Surface Structure means the same as the client's original Surface Structure, then the Surface Structure is semantically ill formed. As an additional example, the client says,

(186) *You bore me.*

To apply the paraphrase test, move the verb in this Surface Structure to the end of the new Surface Structure and put the verb *cause* or *make* in its original position, and insert the verb *feel* or *experience*, yielding,

(187) *You make me feel bored.*

The question now is whether this new Surface Structure and the client's original mean the same thing. In this case, they do, and the client's original Surface Structure is identified as being semantically ill formed. To assist you in training your intuitions in identifying this class of semantically ill-formed Surface Structures, we present the following set of sentences. Determine which of the Surface Structures are ill formed by using the paraphrase test with form (A).

(188) *Music pleases me.* = Music makes me feel pleased.

(189) *My husband likes me.* ≠ My husband makes me feel liked.

(190) *Your ideas annoy me.* = Your ideas make me feel annoyed.

(191) *His plan insults me.* = His plan makes me feel insulted.

(192) *Policemen follow me.*   ≠   Policemen make me
feel followed.

One additional, frequently occurring Surface Structure form in
this class is
(193) *I'm sad that you forgot our anniversary.*
or,
(194) *I'm sad since you forgot our anniversary.*
or,
(195) *I'm sad because you forgot our anniversary.*
Once again, these three Surface Structures can be paraphrased by
the Surface Structure:
(196) *Your forgetting our anniversary makes me feel sad.*
Notice that this last Surface Structure is of the general form (B).
Thus, a paraphrase test is again available here to assist you in
training your intuitions. Specifically, if the client's Surface Structure can be paraphrased by a sentence of the general form (B), it is
semantically ill formed.
We present an additional set of Surface Structures. Determine
which of them are semantically ill formed by using the paraphrase
test with form (B).

(197) *I'm down since you*   =   Your not helping me
won't help me.   makes me feel down.

(198) *I'm lonely because*   =   Your not being here
you're not here.   makes me feel lonely.

(199) *I'm happy that I'm*   =   My going to Mexico
going to Mexico.   makes me feel happy.

(Note: The paraphrase test works but the Surface Structure is not
ill formed since both nouns, X and Y in the general form (B), have
the same referential index.)

(200) *She's hurt that you're*   =   Your not paying any
not paying any atten-   attention to her
tion to her.   makes her feel hurt.

But,
In addition to the forms of Surface Structures which we have
presented involving ways that the client experiences having **no
choice,** we have found it useful in teaching other therapists in
training to hear the cue word *but*. This conjunction *but*, which

translates in many of its uses logically as *and not,* functions to identify what the client considers the reasons or conditions which make something he wants impossible or which make something he doesn't want necessary. For example, the client says:

(201) *I want to leave home but my father is sick.*

When we hear Surface Structures of this form, we understand the client to be identifying a cause-effect relationship in his model of the world. Thus, we call Surface Structures of this general form Implied Causatives.

(202) *X but Y*

In the specific example above, the client is reporting what is a necessary causal connection in his model, namely, that his father's being sick prevents him from leaving home. The portion of the Surface Structure represented by X identifies something the client wants (i.e., *to leave home*) and the portion represented by Y identifies the condition or reason (i.e., *my father is sick*) that the client is blocked from getting X. We have identified one other common form Implied Causatives typically have in Surface Structures. The client says:

(203) *I don't want to leave home, but my father is sick.*

In this form of the Implied Causative the X represents something the client does *not* want (i.e., *to leave home*), and the Y represents the condition or reason that is forcing the client to experience the thing he doesn't want (i.e., *my father is sick*). In other words, the client's father's being sick is forcing the client to leave home. These are the two Implied Causatives that we have most frequently encountered. Both of the forms share the characteristic that the client experiences no choice. In the first case, he wants something (the X in the general form *X but Y*) and some condition is preventing him from getting it (the Y). In the second case, the client does not want something (the X), but something else (the Y) is forcing him to experience it. The following set of Surface Structures is composed of examples of Implied Causatives to assist you in recognizing the semantic relationship.

(204) *I would change but a lot of people depend on me.*

(205) *I don't want to get angry but she is always blaming me.*

(206) *I would like to get to the bottom of this, but I'm taking up too much of the group's time.*

(207) *I don't enjoy being uptight but my job demands it.*

Therapists have at least the following three choices in coping with Implied Causatives.

(a) Accept the cause-effect relationship and ask if it is always that way. For example, the client says:

(205) *I don't want to get angry but she is always blaming me.*

The therapist may respond:

(206) *Do you always get mad when she blames you?*

The client will often recognize times when she has blamed him and he has not gotten angry. This opens up the possibility of determining what the difference is between those times and when her blaming "automatically makes" the client angry.

(b) Accept the cause-effect relationship and ask the client to specify this relationship of Implied Causative more fully. To the client's Surface Structure above, the therapist may respond:

(207) *How, specifically, does her blaming you make you angry?*

The therapist continues to ask for specifics until he has a clear image of the process of Implied Causation as represented in the client's model.

(c) Challenge the cause-effect relationship. One direct way of doing this which we have found useful is to feed back a Surface Structure which reverses the relationship. For example, the client says:

(205) *I don't want to get angry but she's always blaming me.*

The therapist may respond:[7]

(208) *Then, if she didn't blame you, you wouldn't become angry, is that true?*

or, the client says:

(201) *I want to leave home but my father is sick.*

The therapist may respond:

(209) *Then, if your father weren't sick, you would leave home, right?*

This technique amounts to asking the client to reverse the condition in his model which is preventing him from achieving what he wants, or to reverse or remove the conditions in his model which are forcing him to do something he doesn't want to do and then asking whether this reversal gives him what he wants. Let's examine this process more carefully. If someone says to me:

I want to relax but my back is killing me.

I understand him to be saying:

$$I \text{ want to relax but} \begin{Bmatrix} I \text{ can't relax} \\ I \text{ am not relaxed} \end{Bmatrix} \text{because my}$$

back is killing me.

Thus, Surface Structures of the form:
>   *X but Y*

involve a deletion. Their full form is:
>   *X and not X because of Y*

Using the previous example we have the initial Surface Structure:
>   *I want to leave home but my father is sick.*

which, using the equivalence we just suggested, has a full representation:

$$I\ want\ to\ leave\ home\ and\ \begin{Bmatrix} I\ can't \\ I\ don't \end{Bmatrix}\ leave\ home\ because$$

my father is sick.

Once this fuller version of the original Surface Structure is available, the therapist may apply the reversal technique for Implied Causatives. From a Surface Structure of the form
>   *X and not X because of Y*

he forms a new reversed Surface Structure with only the second part of the fuller version:
>   *not X because of Y.*

This new Surface Structure consists of an *If . . . then . . .* construction with this latter portion of the full representation reversed where negatives have been added for both the X and the Y portions. In a step-by-step presentation:

(1) Place the latter portion of the full representation in an *If . . . then . . .* construction in reversed order —

$$If\ (my\ father\ is\ sick),\ then\ (\begin{Bmatrix} I\ can't \\ I\ don't \end{Bmatrix}\ leave\ home).$$

$\{\ \}$ *means one expression* **or** *the other/not both.*

(2) Introduce negatives into both the *If* part and the *then* part —

$$If\ (my\ father\ weren't\ sick),\ then\ (\begin{Bmatrix} I\ can't \\ I\ don't \end{Bmatrix}\ \mathbf{not}$$

leave home).

or, translating the double negatives into grammatical English:

If (my father weren't sick), then ($\left\{\begin{array}{l} I\ could \\ I\ would \end{array}\right\}$ *leave home).*

(3) Present the reversed generalization to the client for verification or denial. *If your father weren't sick, you would leave home?*

This reversal technique has been, in our experience, very effective in challenging the Cause-Effect generalization involved. The client often succeeds in taking responsibility for his continuing decision to do or not to do what he originally claims someone or something else controls. To review, the reversal technique for Implied Causatives of the form *X but Y* involves the following steps:

(1) Expand the client's original Surface Structure to its fuller version (with the deletion restored), using the equivalence:

$$(X \quad but \quad Y) \longrightarrow (X \quad and \quad not \quad X \quad because \quad Y)$$

$$\left(\begin{array}{l} I\ want\ to \\ leave\ home \end{array}\right)\ but\ \left(\begin{array}{l} my\ father \\ is\ sick \end{array}\right) \longrightarrow \left(\begin{array}{l} I\ want\ to \\ leave\ home \end{array}\right)\ and\ \left(\left\{\begin{array}{l} I\ can't \\ I\ don't \end{array}\right\}\ \begin{array}{l} leave \\ home \end{array}\right)\ because\ \left(\begin{array}{l} my\ father \\ is\ sick \end{array}\right)$$

(2) Place the second portion of the restored Surface Structure — the portion after the *and* — in an *If . . . then . . .* construction in the reversed order: (See page 103)

(3) Introduce negatives into the new Surface Structure in both the *If* and the *then* portions: (See page 103)

(2)

$$(not \quad X \quad because \quad Y) \longrightarrow (If \quad Y, \quad then\ not \quad X)$$

$$\left(\left\{\begin{array}{l} I\ can't \\ I\ don't \end{array}\right\} leave\ home\right) because \left(\begin{array}{l} my\ father \\ is\ sick \end{array}\right) \longrightarrow If \left(\begin{array}{l} my\ father \\ is\ sick \end{array}\right) then \left(\left\{\begin{array}{l} I\ can't \\ I\ don't \end{array}\right\} \begin{array}{l} leave \\ home \end{array}\right)$$

(3)

$$(If \quad Y \quad then \quad not \quad X) \longrightarrow (If \quad not \quad Y \quad then \quad not\ not \quad X)$$

$$\left(If \left(\begin{array}{l} my\ father \\ is\ sick \end{array}\right) then \left(\left\{\begin{array}{l} I\ can't \\ I\ don't \end{array}\right\} \begin{array}{l} leave \\ home \end{array}\right)\right) \longrightarrow \left(If \left(\begin{array}{l} my\ father \\ isn't\ sick \end{array}\right)\right) then \left(\left\{\begin{array}{l} I\ can't \\ I\ don't \end{array}\right\} not \begin{array}{l} leave \\ home \end{array}\right)$$

(4) Present the final form of the new Surface Structure as a challenge to the client's original generalization:[6]

Well, then, if your father weren't sick, you would leave home?

(d) One additional technique which we have found useful is to strengthen the client's generalizations about Implied Causative by inserting the modal operator of necessity into the client's Surface Structure when we feed it back, asking the client to verify or challenge it. For example, the client says:

(201) *I want to leave home, but my father is sick.*

The therapist may respond:

(210) *Are you saying that your father's being sick necessarily prevents you from leaving home?*

The client often will balk at this Surface Structure since it blatantly claims that the two events, X and Y, are necessarily connected. If the client balks here, the way is opened for the client and the therapist to explore how it is not necessary. If the client accepts the strengthened version (with *necessarily*), the way is opened for exploring how that necessary causal connection actually works, asking for more specifics about that connection. This technique works particularly well in conjunction with options (a) and (b) described above.

Mind Reading

This class of semantically ill-formed Surface Structures involves the belief on the part of the speaker that one person can know what another person is thinking and feeling without a direct communication on the part of the second person. For example, the client says:

> (211) *Everybody in the group thinks that I'm taking up too much time.*

Notice that the speaker is claiming to know the contents of the minds of all of the people in the group. In the following set of Surface Structures, identify those which contain the claim that one person knows the thoughts or feelings of another person.

(212)	*Henry is angry at me.*	yes
(213)	*Martha touched me on the shoulder.*	no
(214)	*I'm sure she liked your present.*	yes
(215)	*John told me he was angry.*	no
(216)	*I know what makes him happy.*	yes
(217)	*I know what's best for you.*	yes
(218)	*You know what I'm trying to say.*	yes
(219)	*You can see how I feel.*	yes

Another less obvious example of this same class is Surface Structures which presuppose that some person is able to read another's mind. For example,

> (220) *If she loved me, she would always do what I would like her to do.*
>
> (221) *I'm disappointed that you didn't take my feelings into account.*

These two cases of semantic ill-formedness — Cause and Effect and Mind-Reading — can be dealt with by the therapist in essentially the same way. Both of these involve Surface Structures which present an image of some process which is too vague to allow the therapist to form a clear picture of what the client's model is. In the first case, a process is described which claims that one person is performing some action which causes another person to experience some emotion. In the second case, a process is described which claims that one person comes to know what another person is thinking and feeling. In neither case is it given how, specifically, these processes are being accomplished. Thus, the therapist responds by asking, how, specifically, these processes occur. In our experience, Surface Structures which include Cause and Effect and Mind-Reading identify portions of the client's model in which impoverishing distortions have occurred. In Cause and Effect Surface Structures, the clients feel that they literally have no choice, that their emotions are determined by forces outside of themselves. In Mind-Reading Surface Structures, the clients have little choice as they have already decided what the other people involved think and feel. Therefore, they respond on the level of their assumptions about what these others think and feel when, in fact, their assumptions about the others' thoughts and feelings may be invalid. Conversely, in Cause and Effect, the client may come to feel guilty or, at least, responsible for "causing" some emotional response in another. In Mind-Reading clients may systematically fail to express their thoughts and feelings, making the assumption that others are able to know what they are thinking and feeling. We are not suggesting that it is impossible for one human being to come to know what another is thinking and feeling but that we want to know exactly by what process this occurs. Since it is highly improbable that one human being can directly read another's mind, we want details about how this information was transferred. We view this as being very important, as in our experience the client's assumed ability to read another's mind and the client's assumptions that another can read his mind is the source of vast amounts of inter-personal difficulties, miscommunication and its accompanying pain. Even less probable from our experience is the ability of one person to directly and necessarily cause an emotion in another human being. Therefore, we label all Surface Structures of these forms semantically ill formed until the process by which what they claim is true is made explicit, and the Surface Structures representing this process are themselves well formed in therapy. The therapist asks for an explicit account of the process implied by Surface Structures of these two classes essentially by the question *how?* As before, in the section on incompletely specified verbs, the therapist is satisfied only when he has a clearly focused image of the process being described. This process might proceed as follows:

C: *Henry makes me angry.*
T: *How, specifically, does Henry make you angry?*
C: *He never considers my feelings.*

The therapist has at least the following choices:

(a) *What feelings, specifically?*
(b) *How do you know that he never considers your feelings?*

The therapist chooses to ask (b) and the client responds:

C: *Because he stays out so late every night.*

The therapist now has at least the following choices:

    (a) *Does Henry's staying out at night always make you angry?*

    (b) *Does Henry's staying out at night always mean that he never considers your feelings?*

The client's subsequent Surface Structures are subjected to the well-formed-in-therapy conditions by the therapist.

The Lost Performative

Each of us has noticed that in the therapeutic encounter clients characteristically make statements in the form of a generalization about the world itself, which include judgments which we recognize as being true of their model of the world. For example, the client says

    (222) *It's wrong to hurt anyone's feelings.*

We understand this sentence to be a statement about the client's model of the world, specifically, a rule for himself. Notice that the form of the Surface Structure the client uses suggests a generalization which is true about the world; the Surface Structure is not relativized to the client. There is no indication in the Surface Structure that the client is aware that the statement made is true for his particular model; there is no indication that the client recognizes that there may be other possibilities. We translate this sentence, then, into the Surface Structure

    (223) *I say to you that it's wrong for me to hurt anyone's feelings.*

Within the transformational model, linguists have presented an analysis which shows that every Surface Structure is derived from a Deep Structure which has a sentence of the form (see Ross, 1970)

    (224) *I say to you that S*

where S is the Surface Structure. This higher sentence is called the Performative and is, in most cases, deleted by a transformation called Performative Deletion in its derivation to Surface Structures. Notice that, by this analysis, the Deep Structure explicitly identifies the speaker as the source of the generalization about the world; in other words, the sentence which shows up in Surface Structures as a generalization about the world is represented in Deep Structure as a generalization from the speaker's model of the world. The point of this is not to have the client present each Surface Structure preceded by the Performative, but rather to train ourselves as therapists to recognize that the generalizations which the client presents about the world are generalizations about his model of the world. Once recognized, the therapist may challenge these generalizations in such a way that the client comes to see these generalizations as true for his belief system at a specific moment in time. Since these are generalizations about his beliefs, rather than generalizations about the world itself, the therapist may work to assist the client in developing other possible options within his model. This is particularly important in cases in which the generalization reduces the choices experienced by the client. This is typically associated with areas of the client's model in which he experiences pain and has limited options which he does not find satisfying. There are a number of cue words which we have found useful in identifying Surface Structures of this class. These include:

> *good, bad, crazy, sick, correct, right, wrong, only* (as in: *There is only one way. . .) true, false, . . .*

These are only some of the cue words which you may find useful in identifying Surface Structures of this class. The identifying feature of this class is that the Surface Structures have the form of making generalizations about the world; they are not relativized to the speaker. Linguistically, all trace of the Performative has been deleted.

WELL FORMED IN THERAPY

We have presented an extended set of explicit examples which therapists can use to train their intuitions in identifying the phenomenon we called "well formed in therapy." This constitutes the explicit Meta-model for therapy. While we recognize that our Meta-model covers only a portion of the verbal communication which is possible in therapy, we present in the next chapter examples of therapy in which we have restricted the therapist totally to our Meta-model. This is artificial in that the Meta-model is a set of tools designed to be used in conjunction with the different possible approaches to therapy. We want you to imagine the potentially increased effectiveness of therapy conducted with our Meta-model incorporated into your specific approach to therapy. We want to remind you that, while our Meta-model is designed specifically for verbal communication, it is a special case of the general modeling that we, as humans, do. We will generalize our Meta-model to other forms of human representational systems in Chapter Six.

EXERCISE C

Each of the specific sections presented detail steps for you to go through in order to sharpen your intuitions regarding well formed in therapy. All that is required is that you read carefully and apply the step-by-step procedures outlined, and that you have access to some set of Surface Structures. The step-by-step procedures are presented here; the set of Surface Structures to which you may apply these techniques is available wherever people are talking. One specific way of obtaining Surface Structures to use in applying these techniques is to use your own internal voice (inner dialogue) as a source. We suggest that, initially, you use a tape recorder and tape your internal voice by speaking it out loud. Then use the tape as a source for applying the well-formed-in-therapy conditions. After you have had some practice in this, you may simply become aware of the inner dialogue and apply the conditions directly to these sentences without going through a tape recorder. This technique will provide you with a limitless source of sentences which you can use to train yourself.

We cannot overemphasize the need to practice and familiarize yourself with all of the material in Chapter Four. The step-by-step procedure makes this material learnable; whether or not you specifically learn this material will depend upon your willingness to practice. While the step-by-step procedure may at first feel somewhat artificial, after some practice it will become unnecessary for you to proceed in this manner. That is, after training yourself using these explicit methods, you will be able to operate in a rule-governed way, applying the well-formed-in-therapy conditions, without any need to be aware of the step-by-step procedures.

FOOTNOTES FOR CHAPTER 4

1. The general set of transformations which distinguish the derivation of the Surface Structure (30) in the text from the Surface Structure (31) is called Relative Clause Reduction in the linguistic literature. Both (30) and (31) are derived from the same Deep Structure.

2. Notice that the question

What would happen if you failed to take other people's feelings into account?

differs in one important way from the client's Surface Structure that it is derived from

One must take other people's feelings into account.

In the client's Surface Structure, the word *one* occurs as the subject noun argument of the verb *must take.* . . . The word *one* has no referential index. In forming the question, the therapist shifts the subject noun argument of the client's Surface Structure to a noun argument which has a referential index — specifically, the client — i.e., the word *you*. This kind of referential index shift will be treated in more detail in the section *Generalization*.

   3.   We present these two classes of modal operators as separate classes. They are, however, closely connected in the logical systems from which we borrow the terminology. For example, the following equivalence holds logically as well as psychologically:

not possible not (X) = necessary (X)

In English, the logical equivalence of the two distinct Surface Structures:

It is not possible to not be afraid = It is necessary to be afraid.

We separate the two classes for the purposes of presentation.

   4.   Readers familiar with elementary logical systems will recognize this as a case of the substitution rule in, for example, the propositional calculus. The only constraint is that when some term *me* is substituted for some other term *my husband*, then all instances of the term *my husband* must be replaced by the term *me*. The same constraint works well in the context of therapy.

   5.   The reader familiar with the most elementary of the logical systems can verify this formal equivalence using truth tables:

X	Y	X $\vee$ Y	$\sim$ X $\longrightarrow$ Y
T	T	T	T
T	F	T	T
F	T	T	T
F	F	F	F

Thus, the logical equivalence of
   X $\vee$ Y and $\sim$ X $\longrightarrow$ Y.

where $\sim$ = the negation symbol
and $\longrightarrow$ = the implication symbol

In our experience they also have a psychological equivalence.

   6.   Here, in the analysis of verbs which are differentially specified, we suspect that some of the research currently being conducted in Generative Semantics (see McCawley, Lakoff, Grinder and Postal in the bibliography) will be particularly useful in expanding the Meta-model further.

   7.   Readers familiar with logical systems will notice a similarity between parts of the reversal technique for Implied Causatives and the formal rule of

derivation called Contraposition. The transformation of the original Surface Structure into the challenge by the therapist can be represented by the following sequence:

> Line 1: *X but Y*
> Line 2: *X and not X because Y*
> Line 3: *not X because Y*
> Line 4: *not Y and not not X*

Specifically, if the natural language connective *because* were to be interpreted as the logical connective *implies*, then the transformation between Lines 3 and 4 is the formal transformation Contraposition.

Chapter 5

INTO THE VORTEX

In this chapter we will present a series of (example) transcripts with a running commentary. Our point here is to provide for you the opportunity to see the Meta-model in operation. In order to present to you the clearest image of how the Meta-model operates, we have restricted the therapist in these sessions to the use of Meta-model techniques only. This restriction was placed upon the therapist to provide material for this book that would be a clear representation of the Meta-model and should not be taken as a statement by us that digital communication is all a therapist needs to know about. Neither is it a representation of the work that we do or that we would recommend that the therapist do. Rather, this is an opportunity for you to see the Meta-model in action and to see how each response that our clients provide in the form of a Surface Structure is an opportunity for the therapist to proceed in a variety of ways. This means, as you will see, that at any point in therapy you will have a number of relevant techniques available. We would like you to imagine the Meta-model techniques used in the following transcripts integrated with the form of therapy you already use, and to imagine how the Meta-model, in conjunction, could provide a rich set of choices for you as a therapist.

In the running commentary which we provide for the transcript, it is not our purpose to present the way we see the therapist seeing, hearing, feeling, and thinking about what is happening in the therapeutic encounter. We provide the commentary to first, show how what the therapist is doing may be explicitly described in terms of the Meta-model. We are making no claim that the intermediate processes which are stated in our commentary as occurring in the model actually occur in the human beings whose behavior is being modeled.[1] For example, when our commentary points out that the therapist can identify a deletion in the client's Surface Structure by first determining whether he can create another well-formed Surface Structure of English wherein the process word or verb from the client's original Surface Structure appears with more arguments than it has associated with it in the original Surface Structure, and then can subsequently ask for the portion missing from the Deep Structure representation, we are not suggesting that this is, in fact, what the therapist is doing. Further, we are not recommending that you go through these steps. Secondly, in addition to offering the commentary as a way of showing you how verbal behavior in therapy may be understood in terms of the Meta-model, the running commentary will allow you to train and sharpen your intuitions further so that what is described in the commentary in a step-by-step process will become immediate for you. Our experience in training therapists in the Meta-model has been that, typically, they experience a phase in which they become aware that they are going through a step-by-step process. As they perfect this technique, it becomes automatic and drops out of their consciousness. Their behavior, however, is still systematic in this respect.

TRANSCRIPT 1

Ralph is 34 years old and works as assistant manager of a division of a large electronics firm.

The client was asked what he hoped to get out of the interview and began:

(1) **Ralph:** *Well . . . I'm not really sure . . .*

The client is experiencing difficulty saying exactly what it is that he wants. Remember, one of the first tasks of the therapist is to understand the client's model (especially those portions which are impoverishing). The therapist here notices a deletion in the first Surface Structure the client presents. Specifically, he identifies the process or relationship word *sure*, and that the client has provided only one argument or noun *(1)* for the predicate *sure*. The therapist can determine whether this Surface Structure is a full representation of the client's Deep Structure by asking himself whether he can create another well-formed Surface Structure of English with the predicate *sure* and which has more than one argument or noun. For example, the Surface Structure

( ) *I'm sure of the answer.*

In this Surface Structure, there are two arguments or nouns associated with *sure:* someone who is sure of something (in this case, *I*), and something that the person is sure of (in this case, *the answer*). Thus, the therapist knows by his intuitions as a native speaker of English that the client's Deep Structure contained a portion which does not appear in his Surface Structure — it has been deleted. The therapist chooses to try to recover the deleted material by asking for it.

(2) Therapist: *You're not sure of what?*

Therapist asks for missing portion of Deep Structure.

(3) R: *I'm not sure that this will be helpful.*

The client has produced a new Surface Structure containing the information which had been deleted from his first Surface Structure. The therapist listens to the client and examines his new sentence, noticing, (a) an argument or noun *(this)* associated with the verb *will be helpful* which has no referential index; (b) that the Surface Structure representation is incomplete — this predicate *helpful* occurs in well-formed Surface Structures of English with more than one argument or noun (e.g.,

( ) *You are being helpful to me.)*

Since *helpful* can occur with more than one argument noun as it did in the client's Surface Structure, the therapist knows that a portion of the client's Deep Structure has been deleted; (c) that the verb *helpful* is very incompletely specified; the Surface Structure presents the therapist with no clear image of the kind of help the client wants.

By recognizing the specific ways in which the client's Surface Structure fails to be well formed in therapy, the therapist has made a number of options available to himself, such as: (1) he may ask for the referential index — *You're not sure that what, specifically, will be helpful?*, (2) he may ask for the deleted material — *helpful to whom/what?*, (3) he may ask the client what specific kind of help he had hoped for, — *Helpful in what way?*

(4) **T:** *You're not sure what, specifically, will be helpful to whom?*

The therapist has chosen to go for both (1) and (2).

(5) **R:** *Well, I'm not sure that this experiment will be helpful. You see, when I first went to Dr. G., he asked me if I'd be willing to participate in this experiment, . . . and well, I feel that there's something I really*

The client is expressing concern that the experimental conditions — restricting the therapist to the Meta-model techniques — will not allow him to get the help that he wants. The therapist is attempting to understand the client's model and notices the following: (a) the client's first Surface Structure contains the nominalization *experiment* derived from the verb *to experiment;* it has two noun arguments associated with it which have

*need help with
but this is just an
experiment.*

been deleted — the person doing
the experiment and the person or
thing being experimented upon; (b)
in the client's first Surface Structure, one of the arguments of the
verb *helpful* has been deleted (specifically, *helpful to whom*); (c) also,
in the client's first Surface Structure, the verb *helpful* is very incompletely specified — it presents no
clear image; (d) in the latter part of
the client's second Surface Structure, the noun *something* occurs —
this noun has no referential index;
(e) the Surface Structure noun *help*
is a nominalization from the verb
help, is very incompletely specified and has two deletions: it presents no clear image of the person
or thing helping and the person or
thing being helped; (f) again, the
nominalization *experiment* occurs
with both of the deletions mentioned in (a) above; (g) the client's
last Surface Structure in this section is of the general form *X but Y*
— the Implied Causative. Specifically, the implication is that the
client wants something (X = *there's
something that I really want help
with*) and there is something which
is preventing him from getting it,
(Y = *this is just an experiment*).

(6) **T:** *How will this just
being an
experiment
prevent you from
getting the help
that you need?*

The therapist chooses to challenge
the Implied Causative (g).

(7) **R:** *Experiments are
for research, but
there's something*

The client responds with a re-
statement of the Implied Causative,
X but Y. Notice that it still con-

	I really need help with.	tains (a) the old nominalization *experiment* with two deletions; (b) a new nominalization *research* with two deletions — the person doing the research, and the person or thing being researched; (c) the noun *something* which is missing a referential index; and (d) the old nominalization *help* with its two deletions.
(8) T:	*What, specifically, do you really need help with?*	The therapist lets the Implied Causative stand unchallenged and chooses to go after the referential index (c).
(9) R:	*I don't know how to make a good impression on people.*	The client presents a Surface Structure which he sees as providing the referential index for the noun *something* in his last Surface Structure. This new Surface Structure violates the well-formed-in-therapy conditions of (a) the nominalization *impression* with one deletion — the person or thing doing the impressing; (b) the adjective *good* in the phrase *good impression* is derived from a Deep Structure predicate *X is good for Y*, the X in this form is the impression, the Y has been deleted — i.e., who is the impression good for — who benefits from this action; (c) the noun *people* has no referential index; (d) the client's Surface Structure is semantically ill formed as he appears to be mind-reading. He states that he doesn't know how to make a good impression on people but fails to state how he knows that this is true. The way he knows he doesn't make a good impression is not stated.

(10) **T:** *Let me see if I understand you — you are saying that this being just an experiment will necessarily prevent you from finding out how to make a good impression on people. Is that true?*

The therapist chooses to ignore the ill-formedness of the client's new Surface Structure. He chooses instead to re-connect the answer to his question about the referential index back up with the Implied Causative the client presented earlier by simply substituting the answer he received back into his former question. Here he is checking with the client to make sure he understands the client's model and also, by strengthening the client's generalization by inserting a modal operator of necessity, he asks the client to verify or challenge the generalization.

(11) **R:** *Well, . . . I'm not really sure . . .*

The therapist's challenge of the client's generalization is successful — the client begins to waver.

(12) **T:** *(interrupting) Well, are you willing to find out?*

The therapist recognizes that his challenge has succeeded (he hears the client's Surface Structure — Well, I'm not really sure . . .) and moves quickly, asking the client to re-connect his generalization with his actual experience by trying to get the help he needs under these conditions.

(13) **R:** *Yeah, o.k.*

The client agrees to try.

(14) **T:** *Who, specifically, don't you know how to make a good impression on?*

The therapist now returns to the ill-formedness of the client's former Surface Structure above and chooses to go after the referential index missing on *people* in the phrase *a good impression on people.*

(15) **R:** *Well, nobody.*

The client fails to supply the referential index requested by the therapist. The word *nobody* is one of the special class of nouns and phrases which fails to refer as they contain the universal quantifier (logically: nobody = all persons not). The client is now claiming that in his model there is no one on whom he can make a good impression. Thus, the therapist may choose (a) to challenge the generalization, or (b) ask again for the referential index.

(16) **T:** *Nobody? Can you think of anybody on whom you have ever made a good impression?*

The therapist mentions the word with the lack of referential index again and then asks the client to challenge the generalization by asking for an exception.

(17) **R:** *Ah, mmm, . . . yeah, well, some people, but . . .*

Again the challenge works — the client recognizes some exceptions. His partial answer again (a) contains a noun phrase which fails to carry a referential index, and, (b) includes the beginning of a disqualifying *but* phrase.

(18) **T:** *Now then, whom, specifically, don't you know how to make a good impression on?*

The therapist has again been successful in asking the client to challenge his generalization but still has not received a referential index for the noun phrase — he requests it again.

(19) **R:** *. . . I guess what I have been trying to say is that women don't like me.*

The client responds by altering his statement from *I don't know how to make a good impression on people* to *women don't like me.* These two Surface Structures share two well-formedness violations: (a) they each contain a noun which carries no referential index (*people* and *women*), and (b) they each claim that the client is able to know the emotional state of some other human being without presenting the description of how the client knows these things. The client's Surface Structure also contains a deletion associated with the verb *say* — the person to whom the client is saying what he is saying.

(20) T: *Which woman, specifically?*

The therapist chooses to request the referential index again.

(21) R: *Most women I meet.*

The client responds with a noun phrase which also fails to carry a referential index — notice the term *most* which we identified as one of the special set of words and phrases containing quantifiers which therefore fail to refer. The phrase gives no clear image.

(22) T: *Which woman, specifically?*

The therapist requests the referential index again.

(23) R: *Well, most women really . . . but as you said that, I just started to think about this one woman — Janet.*

The client initially failed to provide the referential index requested (i.e., *most women really*) and then provides it — the client identifies the woman in question and names her. Notice that the client's naming a person when the therapist requests a referential index clarifies and greatly focuses the client's model for the client but provides much less for the therapist. In addition, notice that there is a deletion of an argument noun associated with the predicate *think* (i.e., X thinks Y about Z) — specifically, what the client thought about Janet.

(24) T: *Who's Janet?*

The therapist has the referential index but requests information about who this person is in relation to the client. It would, for example, make a difference to the therapist if Janet was the client's mother, daughter, wife, lover, sister, . . . The therapist ignores the deletion in the client's last Surface Structure.

(25) **R:** *She's this woman I just met at work.*

The client supplies some additional information.

(26) **T:** *Now, how do you know that you didn't make a good impression on Janet?*

The therapist is trying to develop a fully focused picture of the client's model of the world for himself. He has succeeded in getting a referential index for an argument noun which originally had no connection with the client's experience. The therapist now integrates this material — the argument noun with the referential index: Janet, the woman the client has just met at work — with the client's original generalization. Thus, the client's original generalization *I don't know how to make a good impression on people* becomes *I don't know how to make a good impression on Janet.* Notice that this new Surface Structure is connected with a specific experience which the client has had — generalizations block change; reconnecting the client's generalization with (at least) one of the experiences on which the generalization was based. The therapist, having integrated this material, begins to question the process of how the client knows that he didn't make a good impression on Janet — this is a choice which the therapist had previously — he now makes this choice and asks the client to describe how he knows that he didn't make a good impression on Janet — challenging what appears to be mind-reading on the part of the client.

(27) **R:** *Well, I just know. . .*

The client fails to specify the process word, the verb, more completely.

(28) **T:** *How, specifically, do you know?*

The therapist again asks the client how he knows, specifically, that he didn't make a good impression on Janet.

(29) **R:** *She just didn't like me.*

Again, the client presents a Surface Structure in which he claims knowledge of another person's inner experience without specifying how he gained that knowledge — apparently mind-reading.

(30) **T:** *How, specifically, do you know that Janet didn't like you?*

The therapist continues to challenge the client's reports of mind-reading.

(31) **R:** *She wasn't interested in me.*

Again, the client claims knowledge of another's inner state.

(32) **T:** *Interested in what way?*

Again, the therapist challenges the mind-reading. Notice that there are two general forms the therapist has available for use in challenging semantically ill-formed Surface Structures which involve mind-reading. Either the form (a) *how do you know X?* where X is the client's Surface Structure (e.g., *she wasn't interested in you.*); or, as the therapist uses in this case, the form (b) Verb in what way/manner? where Verb is the verb from the client's original Surface Structure (e.g., *interested*). Both questions request that the client specify how the process occurred — essentially, a request to specify the process word or verb more completely.

(33) **R:** *She didn't pay attention to me.*

For the fourth successive time, the client provides a Surface Structure which involves mind-reading.

(34) **T:** *How didn't she pay attention to you?*

The therapist again challenges the client's mind-reading.

(35) **R:** *She didn't look at me.*

The client finally provides a Surface Structure in response to a request to specify a process which appears to be mind-reading, which identifies a situation which is verifiable — doesn't involve a mind-reading claim.

(36) **T:** *Let me see If I understand this. You know that Janet wasn't interested in you because she didn't look at you?*

The therapist substitutes the new non-mind-reading material into a Surface Structure which identifies it as the basis for the mind-reading claims that the client has been making. Here the therapist is checking to see whether he has understood the client's model of his experience. He requests verification from the client.

(37) **R:** *That's right!*

The client verifies the therapist's statement about his model.

(38) **T:** *Is there any way you could imagine Janet not looking at you and her still being interested in you?*

The therapist has offered a generalization and the client has verified it. Now notice the form of that Surface Structure (36): X because Y. The therapist, having had the client verify it, may now challenge this generalization, again asking the client to re-connect his generalization with his experience. The therapist asks the client whether the connection between the X and Y connected by the relation word *because* in the general form *X because Y* always occurs.

(39) R: *Well, ... I don't know...*

The client wavers.

(40) T: *Do you always look at everyone you're interested in?*

The therapist challenges the generalization, again using the same technique — this time shifting the referential indices so that the generalization

> Janet look at you
> You look at everyone

> Janet interested in you
> You interested in everyone

(41) R: *I guess ... not always. But just because Janet is interested in me doesn't mean that she likes me.*

The therapist's challenge to the client's Surface Structure succeeds — the client admits that his generalization is faulty. The next Surface Structure by the client invites the inference that he thinks that Janet doesn't like him. Notice that again the client is claiming knowledge of another's inner state.

(42) T: *How, specifically, do you know that she doesn't like you?*

The therapist again challenges the client's mind-reading by asking the client to specify the process more completely.

(43) R: *She doesn't listen to me.*

The client presents a new Surface Structure, again semantically ill formed (mind-reading). Notice that there is a difference — I can determine whether another is looking at me (note, not seeing me, just looking at me) simply by observing her, but I cannot determine whether another is listening to me by simply observing her (nor can I determine whether she hears me by observing alone).

(44) **T:** *How, specifically, do you know that she doesn't listen to you?*

The therapist challenges the client's mind-reading Surface Structure by asking for a more complete specification of the process.

(45) **R:** *Well, she doesn't ever look at me (beginning to get angry). You know how women are! They never let you know if they notice you.*

The client retreats to the previous well-formed Surface Structure with, notice, the addition of a universal quantifier *ever*. The addition of this quantifier results in a generalization which the therapist may choose to challenge. Furthermore, the client's next Surface Structure presents several options to the therapist: (a) the client's assertion *You know* involves mind-reading; (b) the noun *women* carries no referential index; (c) the Surface Structure does not specify *how women are* — it simply asserts that the therapist knows. The process word or verb *are* is completely unspecified. The client's next Surface Structure fails (at least) two well-formed-in-therapy conditions: (a) the noun *they* occurs twice in the Surface Structure — it has no referential index,[2] and (b) the universal quantifier *never* identifies a generalization which may be challenged.

(46) **T:** *Like who, specifically?*

The therapist chooses to go after the referential index.

(47) **R:** *(angry) Like my mother . . . ah, God damn it! She never was*

The client identifies the missing referential index. The client's next Surface Structure has the same form as the previous Surface Struc-

	interested in me.	tures (31, 36, 38, 41) — this time, however, the pronoun *she* refers to the client's mother, not Janet. The Surface Structure is semantically ill formed, as before, as the process by which the client has come to know that his mother wasn't interested in him is not specified.
(48) T:	*How do you know that your mother was never interested in you?*	The therapist challenges the client's Surface Structure, asking for a more fully specific process description.
(49) R:	*Every time I tried to show her that I cared about her, she never noticed it (begins to sob) . . . why didn't she notice?*	The client's Surface Structure includes (a) two universal quantifiers (*every time* and *never*), thus identifying a generalization which the therapist may choose to challenge, and (b) three process words or verbs which are very incompletely specified (*show, care about, notice*) as they do not present a clear image to the therapist, and (c) one claim to knowledge of another's inner perception without specifying the process (*notice* in *she never noticed . . .*).
(50) T:	*How, specifically, did you try to show her that you cared about her?*	The therapist now begins to clarify the image for himself by asking for a more fully specified description of the process. He chooses to ask first about the client's actions.
(51) R:	*(sobbing softly) Like all the time I used to come home from school and do things for her.*	This Surface Structure by the client contains (a) a universal quantifier *all the time* subject to challenge by the therapist, and (b) a noun argument *things* which has no referential index.
(52) T:	*What things, specifically, did*	The therapist continues to explore the client's model, specifically

you do for her?

attempting to get a clear image of the client's perception of his actions. He selects option (b).

(53) **R:** *Well, I always used to clean up the living room and wash the dishes . . . and she never noticed . . . and never said anything.*

The client's Surface Structure offers the therapist the following four options: (a) three universal quantifiers *(always, never, never)*, identifying three challengeable generalizations in the client's model; (b) the occurrence of the very incompletely specified verb *notice;* (c) a claim by the client of knowledge of another's perceptions *(notice);* (d) a deletion associated with the verb *say* (i.e., to whom?). In addition, notice the way the client first states *she never noticed,* then pauses and says, *she never said anything.* In our experience, two successive Surface Structures with the same syntactic form (i.e., noun—quantifier—verb. . .) separated only by a pause, identify two sentences which, for the speaker, are equivalent or nearly equivalent in meaning in the client's model. As in this case, such equivalences are very useful in coming to understand the connections between the client's experience and the way that experience is represented. For example, notice that the first of these two statements is a claim that the client has knowledge of another's perception while the second is semantically well formed, involving no mind-reading. If, in fact, the two statements are equivalences, the second one identifies the experience which is represented by the first (a semantically ill-formed Surface Structure), or, in other words, in the client's model, the client's mother's not saying anything is equivalent to her not noticing.

(54) T: *Ralph, does your mother's not saying anything to you about what you used to do mean that she never noticed what you had done?*

The therapist has chosen to ignore the well-formed-in-therapy violations in the client's Surface Structure for the time being and checks to see whether the last two Surface Structures are, in fact, equivalences. Such generalizations are extremely important in coming to understand the client's experience.

(55) R: *Yeah, since she never noticed what I did for her, she wasn't interested in me.*

The client verifies the equivalence and supplies a third Surface Structure which, since it is substituted for one of the other two (specifically, *she didn't say anything*) is also equivalent. This third Surface Structure is: *she wasn't interested in me.* The client's Surface Structure also includes a universal quantifier *never*.

(56) T: *Let me get this straight: you're saying that your mother's not noticing what you did for her means that she wasn't interested in you?*

The therapist decides to verify the equivalence of these two Surface Structures.

(57) R: *Yes, that's right.*

The client again verifies the generalization involved.

(58) T: *Ralph, have you ever had the experience of someone's doing something for you and you didn't notice*

The therapist decides to challenge the client's generalization — here he chooses to begin the challenge by shifting the referential indices. (See page 128)
and therefore, the generalizations are transformed: (See page 128)

*until after they
pointed it out
to you?*

| *you (the client)*
↓ *someone/they*

| *your (client's) mother*
↓ *you (the client)*

| *your mother didn't notice . . .*
↓ *you didn't notice . . .*

and

| *you do something for your
mother*
↓ *someone do something for you*

Notice that the effect of shifting the referential indices in this way is to place the client in the position of the active member of his original generalization — his mother, the person he is criticizing.

(59) R: *Well, . . ., yeah, I remember one time . . .*

The client at first hesitates, then admits that he has been in the position that he described his mother occupying in his original generalization.

(60) T: *Did you not notice what they had done for you because you weren't interested in them?*

The therapist, having received the admission by the client that he has had this experience, interrupts him and asks if the equivalence

X not notice $=$ X not interested

is valid when he is the one who did not notice (i.e., X = the client), thereby challenging the generalization.

(61) R: *No, I just didn't notice. . .*

The client denies this equivalence when he is the person not noticing.

(62) T: *Ralph, can you imagine that your mother just didn't notice*

The therapist, having received a denial of the equivalence

X not notice $=$ X not interested

when X = the client, now reverses

when. . . .	the referential indices that he had shifted earlier. This results in the client's original equivalence statement: namely, that X *not noticing* $= X$ *not interested* *where* $X =$ *client's mother*
(63) R: *No, it's not the same.*	The client recognizes the therapist's challenge before he completes it, interrupts him, and denies that the two cases (where $X =$ the client and where $X =$ the client's mother) are the same. The Surface Structure he uses to deny this fails the well-formed-in-therapy conditions: (a) the pronoun *it* has no referential index, and (b) the second portion of the comparative has been deleted.
(64) T: *It? What's not the same as what?*	The therapist asks for both the referential index and the missing portion of the comparative.
(65) R: *My not noticing is not the same as my mother not noticing — see, she NEVER noticed what I did for her.*	The client fills in the information requested by the therapist. He then goes on to describe the difference between the two cases, namely, that his mother *never* noticed. This universal quantifier identifies a challengeable generalization.
(66) T: *Never?*	The therapist challenges the universal quantifier.
(67) R: *Well, not very many times.*	The client admits that there were exceptions, thereby coming closer to re-connecting his generalization with his experience.
(68) T: *Ralph, tell me about one specific time when your*	The therapist attempts to get the client to focus the model by asking for a specific exception to the client's initial generalization.

> *mother noticed
> what you had
> done for her.*

(69) R:	*Well, once when
... yeah
(angrily), I even
had to tell her.*	One of the argument nouns associated with the verb *tell* has been deleted (tell what?).
(70) T:	*Had to tell her
what?*	The therapist asks for the missing piece of the Surface Structure.
(71) R:	*That I had done
this thing for her.
If she had been
interested enough
she would have
noticed it herself.*	The first Surface Structure includes a noun argument *(this thing)* and lacks a referential index. The client's second Surface Structure includes a deletion associated with the word *enough (enough for what),* and a pronoun *it* without a referential index.
(72) T:	*Interested enough
for what?*	The therapist asks for the deleted material.
(73) R:	*Interested enough
to show me that
she loved me.*	The client supplies the deleted material that the therapist requested. This new Surface Structure includes (a) a violation of the semantic well-formedness condition of mind-reading — the client claims to know whether his mother loved him without specifying how he got that information; (b) the verb *love* is very incompletely specified.
(74) T:	*Ralph, how did
you show your
mother that you
loved her?*	The therapist is attempting to gain a clear image of the way that the client and his mother communicated their feelings of caring for one another. He has been informed by the client that his mother wasn't interested enough to show him that she loved him. The therapist decides to employ the referential

index shift technique. Specifically, he makes the substitution

$$\downarrow \begin{array}{l} your\, mother \\ you\, (the\, client) \end{array} \quad \downarrow \begin{array}{l} you\, (the\, client) \\ your\, mother \end{array}$$

Thus, the portion of the client's last Surface Structure is transformed
> *your mother show you that she loved you*
>
> *you show your mother that you loved her*

Having made this shift in referential indices, the therapist asks the client to focus the image, asking for a more completely specified verb.

(75) **R:** *By doing things for her.*

The client presents a further specification of the verb, setting up the equivalence
> *X loves Y = X do things for Y*
> *where X = the client and*
> *Y = the client's mother*

(76) **T:** *Ralph, did your mother ever do things for you?*

The therapist now shifts the referential indices back to the original Surface Structure (73), and presents one half of the equivalence for the client's verification.

(77) **R:** *Yes, but she never really . . . never let me know for sure.*

The client agrees that his mother did do things for him, but he denies that the equivalence holds — that is,
> *X loves Y ≠ X do things for Y*
> *where X = the client's mother*
> *Y = the client*

The client's new Surface Structure presents the therapist with the following options: (a) ask for the difference in the two situations which makes the equivalence fail to hold (identified by the cue word *but*); (b) there are two occurrences of the challengeable universal quantifier *never;* (c) a deletion associated with the verb *know* (i.e., know what?); (d) a very incompletely specified verb *know.*

(78) **T:** *Never let you know what?*

The therapist chooses option (c) and asks for the deleted noun argument associated with the verb *know.*

(79) **R:** *She never let me know for sure if she really loved me (still sobbing softly).*

The client supplies the missing noun argument. His Surface Structure includes (a) a challengeable universal quantifier *never;* (b) two very incompletely specified verbs *know* and *love.*

(80) **T:** *Did you ever let her know for sure that you loved her?*

The therapist again chooses to use the referential index shift technique. The substitution that he uses is the same as the one that he employed in (74).

(81) **R:** *She knew . . .*

The client's Surface Structure contains (a) a deletion associated with the verb *know;* (b) a violation of the semantic well-formedness condition, mind-reading; (c) a very incompletely specified verb *know.*

(82) **T:** *How do you know she knew?*

The therapist chooses option (c).

(83) **R:** *I . . . I . . . I guess I don't.*

The client wavers, and then admits that he is not able to specify the process by which his mother was supposed to have been able to know that he loved her. This is equivalent to stating that the process in his model is not specified.

(84) *T:* *What prevents you from telling her?*

The client has been unable to identify the process by which his mother was supposed to have been able to know that he loved her. The therapist immediately moves to the technique of asking what is it that prevents the client from using the most direct way he knew of communicating his feelings of love to his mother.

(85) R: *ummm...*
ummm, maybe
nothing.

The client wavers, considering the obvious. His Surface Structure includes a very qualified *maybe* and the universal quantifier *nothing.*

(86) T: *MAYBE?*

The therapist works to get more of a commitment from the client.

(87) R: *I guess I could.*

The client admits the possibility.

(88) T: *Ralph, do you*
guess you could
also tell Janet
how you feel
about her?

The therapist now shifts referential indices again

client's mother
↓
Janet

and asks for a commitment from the client to change the communication process in that relationship so that it is more direct and requires no mind-reading.

(89) R: *That's a little*
scary.

The client hesitates; his Surface Structure contains (a) a noun argument without a referential index *that;* (b) a deletion of the noun argument associated with the verb scary (i.e., scary to whom?).

(90) T: *What is a little*
scary?

The therapist asks for the missing referential index.

(91) R: *That I could just*
go up and tell
her.

The client supplies the missing index and expresses doubt about the communication commitment that the therapist is asking for.

(92) **T:**	*What stops you?*	The therapist uses the technique of asking for the generalization, the outcome of the client's action which he finds scary.
(93) **R:**	*Nothing, that's what's so scary. (laughing)*	The client recognizes that he has that choice.

The therapist at this point moved into non-Meta-model techniques, setting up a contract with Ralph to insure that the new possibilities which he had discovered would be acted upon.

TRANSCRIPT 2

This transcript session took place with a group of trainees who were witnessing a demonstration. Beth is a woman of about 28. She has been married once and has two small children. The demonstration begins:

(1) **B:**	*What should I do first?*	The client begins by requesting direction from the therapist.
(2) **T:**	*Tell me what you are doing here; you said in the interview you wanted some help with something (referring to a two-minute interview an hour before in which five people were chosen for this demonstration).*	The therapist begins by asking the client to specify what she is doing here and, referring to a previous conversation, asks her to verify and explain her request for help.
(3) **B:**	*Let's see, what am I doing here . . . I . . . I want help with . . . well, it's my roommates.*	The client sounds hesitant, somewhat confused; (a) she leaves a Surface Structure uncompleted — *help with* . . ., pauses, then states . . . *it's my roommates.* The verb *help* is very incompletely specified; (b) the nouns *it* and *roommates* have no referential indices.

(4) **T:** *Roommates? . . .*

The therapist decides to ask for a referential index on the noun argument *roommates.*

(5) **B:** *(Interrupting) Karen and Sue, they share the house with me. We also have four children between us.*

The client supplies referential indices as requested by the therapist. She adds more information, thus allowing the therapist a somewhat clearer image of her model.

(6) **T:** *What kind of help would you like with these two people?*

The therapist makes the assumption that the noun argument *roommates* fits in the noun argument position of the sentence that the client left incomplete in her second comment. Presupposing this, the therapist returns to the client's original Surface Structure and asks the client to further specify the process word *help.*

(7) **B:** *They don't seem to understand me.*

The client ignores the therapist's specific question and begins to describe her roommates. Notice that (a) the dative argument associated with the verb *seem* is missing/deleted; (b) the client is claiming knowledge of the inner experience of others without specifying how she got that information — a well-formed-in-therapy violation called mind-reading; (c) the client's Surface Structure includes the very unspecified verb *understand.*

(8) **T:** *How do you know they don't understand you?*

The therapist challenges the client's Surface Structure for violating the semantic well-formedness condition (mind-reading). He asks the client to describe how she came to know how they don't understand her.

(9) **B:** *I guess, it's that they're too busy. . . .*

The client's response fails to be well formed in therapy as: (a) the noun argument *it* has no referential index and, (b) the predicate *too busy* has a deletion associated with it *(too busy for what?)*.

(10) **T:** *Too busy for what?*

The therapist asks for the deleted portion of the client's last Surface Structure.

(11) **B:** *Well . . . too busy to see that I have needs.*

The client supplies the missing material in the form of a new Surface Structure. The new Surface Structure includes a noun argument with no referential index *(needs)*. This particular noun argument is a nominalization from the Deep Structure predicate *to need*.

(12) **T:** *What needs?*

The therapist asks for the referential index on the client's nominalization *needs*.

(13) **B:** *That I would like for them to do something for me once in a while.*

The client's new Surface Structure again lacks a referential index on what she wants from her roommates *(something* in *for them to do something).* The verb *do* is nearly as incompletely specified as possible.

(14) **T:** *Such as what?*

The therapist continues to ask for the missing referential index.

(15) **B:** *They really have a lot of things to do, but sometimes I feel that they are insensitive.*

Again, the client fails to respond to the question from the therapist.[3] Her new Surface Structure is in violation of the well-formed-in-therapy conditions (a) missing referential index on . . . *a lot of things* . . . ; (b) missing referential index on *sometimes;* (c) the almost completely unspecified verb *do* in . . . *things to do* . . . ; (d) a missing dative noun argument associated with the verb *insensitive* (i.e., *insensitive to whom?*); (e) by using the verb *insensitive*, the client is claiming knowledge of the inner state of another without specifying the process by which she knows — mind-reading.

(16) **T**:	*Whom are they insensitive to?*	The therapist asks for the missing noun argument associated with the verb *insensitive* [in Deep Structure, option (d) in above].
(17) **B**:	*Me. And. . .*	The client supplies the missing argument and begins something else.
(18) **T**:	*In what way are they insensitive to you?*	The therapist interrupts, choosing to ask the client to specify how she knows the others involved are insensitive to her — option (e).
(19) **B**:	*You see, I do a lot of things for them, but they don't seem to do anything for me.*	Again the client fails to respond directly to the therapist's question. Her new Surface Structure violates the following well-formed-in-therapy conditions: (a) missing referential index on *a lot of things* and *anything;* (b) the nearly completely unspecified verb *do* occurs twice in the client's Surface Structure; (c) a challengeable universal quantifier in *anything;* (d) a deleted dative noun argument associated with the verb *seem — seem to whom?*
(20) **T**:	*What don't they do for you? What needs don't they see that you have?*	The therapist asks for a couple of the missing referential indices on noun arguments that are floating around — the *anything,* from the client's Surface Structure (19) and the *needs* from the client's Surface Structure (11).

(21) **B:** *I'm a person, too, and they don't seem to recognize that.*[4]

The client continues to fail to respond to the therapist's question. The new Surface Structure contains (a) a presupposition carried by the word *too* at the end of the Surface Structure *I'm a person*. The implication is that someone else (unidentified) is a person — hence, no referential index; (b) a deleted dative noun argument associated with the verb *seem* — *(seem to whom?)*; (c) the client is claiming knowledge of the inner state of another (*. . . they don't seem to recognize . . .*) without stating how she got this information; (d) a relatively incompletely specified verb *recognize.*

(22) **T:** *How don't they recognize that you're a person?*

The therapist is trying to get an image clear to him of the client's model — he keeps returning to the specification of what the roommates actually do — just as he did with (10), (14), (18), (20), and this request. The therapist challenges the ill-formedness of the relatively incompletely specified verb *recognize.*

(23) **B:** *They, both of them, never do anything for me.*

The client responds to the therapist with a Surface Structure which can be challenged on the grounds of: (a) a universal quantifier — *never*, identifying a generalization; (b) a noun argument associated with the general verb *do*, lacking a referential index — *anything*; (c) the nearly completely unspecified pro-verb[5] *do.*

(24) **T:** *They NEVER do ANYTHING for you?*

The therapist chooses to challenge the generalization. He does it by emphasizing (voice quality) the universal quantifiers in the client's original Surface Structure when feeding the sentence back to the client for verification or denial.

(25) B: *No, not never, but I always do things for them whether they ask or not.*

The therapist's challenge to the client's last generalization is successful (i.e., *No, not never*). She goes on to state a new generalization identified by: (a) the universal quantifier *always;* and containing (b) a noun argument without a referential index — *things,* (c) the nearly completely unspecified verb *do,* (d) the deletion of two noun arguments associated with the verb *ask (ask for/about what?* and *ask whom).* Remember, the therapist is still trying to find out who is doing what specifically for whom — what the client means when she says that her roommates fail to recognize her as a person.

(26) T: *Let me see if I understand at this point. If someone recognizes that you are a person, then they will always do things for you whether you ask or not?*

The therapist thinks that he has identified a generalization — specifically, an equivalence between

$$X \text{ not recognize } Y \atop \text{ as a person} = {X \text{ do things for} \atop Y \text{ whether } Y \atop \text{ asks or not}}$$

He puts the generalization in the form of an equivalence generalization and asks the client to confirm or deny it.

(27) B: *Well, maybe not always, . . .*

The client balks at the generalization.

(28) T: *I'm a bit confused at this point; could you tell me what*

The therapist returns to attempting to find out what, specifically, the client's roommates do that the client represents as not recognizing

those things are that they would do if they recognized that you're a person?	her as a person as he did in (22) and (26). He admits he is confused by what the client has said.
(29) B: *You know, like help with the dishes or babysitting, or just anything.*	The client begins to clarify the image by mentioning some concrete things such as *help with the dishes* and *babysitting.* She then throws it away with the noun argument *anything.*
(30) T: *Could you also explain how your roommates are supposed to know what these things are that you want done?*	The therapist has been asking repeatedly how the client knows what her roommates recognize (8), (18), and (20). Here, he makes a referential index shift and asks how (by what process) the client's roommates come to know what the client herself wants.[6]
(31) B: *If they were sensitive enough, they would know.*	The client responds in the patterned way we have seen already, specifically claiming that her roommates can know what she wants without specifying by what process they get this information. In addition, the client's Surface Structure includes well-formedness-condition violations: (a) deletion of a noun argument associated with the verb *sensitive (sensitive to whom?);* (b) a comparative deletion associated with the cue word *enough* in *sensitive enough* (i.e., *sensitive enough for what?);* (c) the deletion of a noun argument associated with the verb *know* (i.e., *know what?).*
(32) T: *Sensitive enough to whom?*	The therapist chooses to ask for one of the deleted arguments — option (a) in (31).

(33) **B:**   *To me.*

The client supplies the missing noun argument requested by the therapist, relativizing the sensitivity (or rather, lack of it) of her roommates to her.

(34) **T:**   *If they were sensitive enough to you, then they should be able to read your mind?*

The therapist now back-tracks to the client's Surface Structure (31) and challenges its semantic ill-formedness (mind-reading), option (d) in (31), directly by explicitly stating the assumption implicit in the client's sentence (31).

(35) **B:**   *Read my mind?*

The client appears confused, taken aback by the therapist's explicit statement of her mind-reading assumption.

(36) **T:**   *Yes, how else could they know what you need and want? Do you tell them?*

The therapist continues to challenge the client's very incomplete description of the process by which her roommates are supposed to know what she wants and needs, trying to get a clear image of the client's model (the therapist's question refers back to the client's Surface Structures (11), (13), and (19). The therapist at this point even offers one possible way that the process he's trying to get a clear image of might occur — *Do you tell them?*

(37) **B:**   *Well, not exactly . . .*

The client denies that she lets her roommates know by telling them directly.

(38) **T:**   *Not exactly how?*

The therapist continues to push for a description of the process.

(39) **B:**   *Well I kinda hint.*

The client's Surface Structure has (a) a deleted noun argument associated with the verb *hint* — (i.e., *hint at what?*); (b) the verb *hint* alone yields no clear image of how the client's roommates are supposed to know what she wants and needs; the already incompletely specified verb *hint* in combination with the qualifier *kinda* makes the image even vaguer; (c) a second deleted noun argument associated with the verb *hint* (i.e., *hint to whom?*).

(40) T: *How do you kinda hint?*

The therapist decides to ask for a more complete specification of the process of *hinting* — option (b) in (39).

(41) B: *I do things for them.*

The client states more completely the process of how she lets her roommates know what she wants and needs — how she kinda hints — that is, she does things for them. The new Surface Structure fails to be well formed in therapy as (a) it includes a noun argument which has no referential index — *things;* (b) it includes the nearly completely unspecified verb *do;* (c) this Surface Structure may be equivalent in the client's model — that is,

$$(X \text{ kinda hints} = (X \text{ does things} \\ \text{to } Y) \qquad \text{for } Y)$$

(42) T: *Then, since you do things for them, they're supposed to know that you want them to do something in return?*

The therapist decides to check to see whether the client will verify this generalization [option (c) in (41)] by repeating the entire generalization to the client.

(43) B: *It sounds sorta funny when you say it like that.*

As the client says, the generalizations from her own model when presented to her by the therapist in a single statement sound funny; she wavers, not willing to verify the generalization. She uses the very incompletely specified verb *funny*.

(44) **T:** *Sort of funny how?*

The therapist asks her to further specify her verb *funny*.

(45) **B:** *Like I'm not being honest or something, but you just can't go around demanding things all the time or people will not want to give them to you.*

The client's Surface Structure includes violations of the following well-formed-in-therapy conditions: (a) a missing referential index on *something;* (b) a missing referential index on *you* (twice); (c) a missing referential index on *all the time;* (d) a missing referential index on *things;* (e) a missing referential index on *people;* (f) incompletely specified verbs *being honest* and *demand;* (g) a challengeable universal quantifier *all* in . . . *all the time;* (h) a modal operator of possibility *can't* in . . . *you can't go;* (i) a mind-reading semantic ill-formed violation in *people will not want* where the client claims to be able to know an inner state of others without specifying how she gets that information; (j) the cue word *but* which identifies a possible Implied Causative; (k) a missing noun argument associated with *demand (demand from whom?)*.

(46) **T:** *Wait a second; who can't go around demanding things all the time from whom?*

The therapist seems to be overwhelmed by the abundance of choices — he decides to ask for two of the violations — a referential index [option (b) in 45] and a missing noun argument [option (k) in (45)].

(47) **B:** *I can't go around demanding things*

The client's Surface Structure includes both of the items requested *from Sue and Karen or they won't want to give me anything.*

by the therapist *[who* (46) *I; from whom* (46) *Karen and Sue].* In addition, her Surface Structure contains (a) modal operator of impossibility; (b) noun arguments with missing referential indices *things* in . . . *go around demanding things,* and *anything* in . . . *give me anything;* (c) a mind-reading violation; the client claims knowledge of an inner state (not only an inner state but a future inner state as well — crystal ball mind-reading) in the phrase . . . *they won't want to;* (d) two unspecified verbs *demand* and *give* which present a very vague, unfocused image of the process. Notice, also, the overall form of the client's Surface Structure — X or Y where X contains a modal operator. In the section on modal operators, we pointed out that one technique for challenging generalizations involving modal operators in the form of sentences such as

I can't . . .

or

It's impossible . . .

or

One may not . . .

is to ask the question, *or what?* Here the client has already supplied the outcome or consequence; that is, the *or what* part — *or Y;* specifically, . . . *or they won't want to;* thereby identifying a full generalization in her model which may be challenged.

(48) **T:** *I thought you said that they didn't give you anything anyway.*

The therapist chooses to challenge the client's generalization. He does this by first translating the client's generalization into an equivalent form. The client says

X or Y: (I don't ask) or (they won't want to give)

As described in Chapter 4, Surface Structures of this form are equivalent to

If not X, then Y: If (I don't ask) then (they won't want to give)

or

If (I ask) then (they won't want to give)

The client's generalization now has the form

If I ask, they won't want to give. . . .

Since the client has already told the therapist both that she doesn't ask (36), (37), (38), (39), (40), and (41), and that they don't give her what she wants or needs (11), (13), (15), (19), and (23), he knows that the reverse of the client's generalization is true in her experience; namely

If I don't ask, they won't want to give. . . .

He, therefore, sees that the *If* part of the generalization is irrelevant, substitutes the word *anyway*, and presents this to the client for her verification or denial.

(49) **B:** *Well, they do sometimes, but not when I want it.*

The therapist's challenge works; the client denys her generalization. Her new Surface Structure includes: (a) two elements which lack referential indices — *sometimes* and *it;* (b) a very incompletely specified verb *do;* (c) the cue word *but.*

(50) **T:** *Do you ask them when you want something?*

The therapist is still trying to get a clear image of how the client and her two roommates communicate

to one another what they want and
need. He asks her specifically
whether she asks them when she
wants something.

(51) B:	*(pause) . . . (Puts her hands in her lap and her face in her hands). Mui. . .kannnt (mumbling).*	The client is experiencing a strong emotion.
(52) T:	*(Softly, but directly) Beth, do you ask when you want something?*	The therapist persists in his attempt to get a clear image of the process by which the client expresses her needs and wants. He repeats the question.
(53) B:	*I can't*	The client uses a modal operator of impossibility, leaving off the remainder of the sentence.
(54) T:	*What prevents you?*	The therapist has now identified an important portion of the client's model. Here the client experiences no choice (53) and a great deal of pain (51). The therapist begins to challenge the limiting portion of the client's model by asking what, specifically, makes this impossibility for her impossible.
(55) B:	*I just can't,. . . I JUST CAN'T*	The client simply repeats that it is not possible for her to ask — she again indicates that she has strong emotions in this area of her model by her changing voice quality and volume.
(56) T:	*Beth, what would happen if you asked for something when you want it?*	The therapist continues to challenge the impoverishing portion of the client's model. He shifts to another of the Meta-model techniques described under modal

operators, asking for an outcome.

(57) **B:** *I can't because people will feel pushed around if I ask for things from them.*

The client is willing to give the outcome. There are several violations of the well-formed-in-therapy conditions in her Surface Structure which may be challenged; (a) the modal operator *can't;* (b) the Cause-Effect relationship *X because Y* identified by the word *because;* (c) noun arguments with no referential indices, *people* and *things;* (d) a crystal-ball mind-reading violation . . . *people will feel pushed;* (e) a deletion noun argument associated with the verb *pushed around* — *pushed around by whom?*

(58) **T:** *Do people ask for things from you?*

The therapist is going to challenge the necessity of the Cause-Effect relationship or generalization which the client has in her model. He begins by shifting referential indices

$$\begin{vmatrix} I \ (the \ client) \\ people \end{vmatrix} \quad \begin{vmatrix} people \\ I \ (the \ client) \end{vmatrix}$$

Thus, the part of the generalization that the therapist is focusing on shifts

$$\begin{vmatrix} I \ ask \ for \ things \ from \ people. \\ People \ ask \ for \ things \ from \ me. \end{vmatrix}$$

Having made the shift, he presents the client with the result for verification or denial.

(59) **B:** *Yes.*

The client verifies that she has had the experience.

(60) **T:** *Do you always feel pushed around?*

The referential index shift which the therapist began in (58) continues as he uses the same shift

I (the client)	people
people	I (the client)

Thus, the other portion of the client's original generalization becomes

| People feel pushed around . . . |
| I feel pushed around . . . |

The therapist now presents this piece of the transformed original Surface Structure, challenging it by emphasizing the universality of the claim with his voice quality emphasis on the universal quantifier *always*.

(61) **B:** *No, not always, but sometimes I do.*

The client denies that the Cause-Effect relationship is necessary [option (b) under (57)]. Her new Surface Structure can be challenged on (a) missing referential index on *sometimes;* (b) nearly completely specified verb *do* or under the assumption that the pro-verb *do* refers back to *pushed around,* then the missing noun argument *pushed around by whom,* and a relatively unspecified verb *pushed around;* (c) the cue word *but.*

(62) **T:** *Beth, are you aware that thirty minutes ago you came to me and asked if I would work with you? You asked for something for yourself?*

Instead of pursuing any of the violations of the well-formed-in-therapy conditions in the client's last Surface Structure, the therapist continues to challenge the Cause-Effect generalization [option (b) in (57)]. The therapist shifts the referential indices of the original generalization. (See page 149)

The therapist has relativized the client's generalization to the ongoing present in therapy. He calls

You (the client)	people
You (the client)	me (the therapist).

The result is:

You (the client) asked for something from people.

You asked for something from me (the therapist).

her attention to this, an experience which contradicts the client's generalization. The therapist asks her to verify or deny this experience.

(63) **B:** *(pause) Yesssss*

The client verifies her experience.

(64) **T:** *Did I feel pushed around?*

The therapist invites the client to check out the remainder of her original Cause-Effect relationship [option (b) in (57)] with an exercise in reading the therapist's mind.

(65) **B:** *I don't think so.*

The client avoids the mind-reading while checking out the remainder of her generalization.

(66) **T:** *Then, could you imagine asking for something for yourself from one of your roommates and their not feeling pushed around?*

The therapist has succeeded in getting the client to deny the generalization in her model which is causing her dissatisfaction and pain (a) by shifting referential indices so that she recalls experiences she herself has had where she didn't feel pushed around when other people asked her for things, and (b) by connecting her generalization with her immediate experience in therapy. He now shifts referential indices again, this time back to the original difficulty the client has with her roommates. He first asks her if she can fantasize an exception to her original generalization with her roommates specifically.

(67) B:	*Yes, maybe.*	The client verifies this possibility.
(68) T:	*Would you like to try?*	The therapist moves to gain the client's commitment to an exception to her original generalization in actual experience as well as fantasy.
(69) B:	*Yes, I would.*	The client indicates that she is willing to try an actual experiment with her roommates.
(70) T:	*And how will you know if your roommates feel pushed around?*	The therapist, having received the client's commitment, returns to the central part of his image of the client's model which he has not yet clarified for himself — the process by which the client and her roommates let one another know what they each want and need — the same process he was trying to clarify in (8), (18), (22), (30), (34), (36), (40), and (42).
(71) B:	*Both of them would probably tell me.*	The client supplies the information which clarifies the therapist's image of her model of how her roommates communicate to her how they're feeling.
(72) T:	*Beth, do you tell people when you feel pushed around?*	The therapist now goes after the other half of the communication process: how she lets them know how she is feeling, what she wants.
(73) B:	*Not exactly, but I let them know.*	The client's Surface Structure includes (a) a deletion of a noun argument associated with the verb *know*; (b) a very poorly specified verb phrase *let know*; (c) the cue word *but*.

(74) **T:** *How do you let them know?*

The therapist, who is still trying to get a clear image of how the client communicates her feelings to her roommates, challenges the poorly specified verb phrase.

(75) **B:** *I guess just by the way I act; they should be able to tell.*

The new Surface Structure includes violations of the following well-formed-in-therapy conditions: (a) referential index missing *the way;* (b) a very incompletely specified verb *act;* (c) a very incompletely specified verb phrase *be able to tell;* (d) a deletion of one of the noun arguments associated with the verb *tell (to tell what?);* (e) the cue word *should.*

(76) **T:** *How? Are they supposed to be able to read your mind again?*

The therapist persists in demanding the specifics of the communication from the client to her roommates.

(77) **B:** *Well, no.*

The client denies that her roommates should be able to read her mind.

(78) **T:** *What stops you from telling them directly that you don't want to do something or that you feel pushed around?*

The therapist chooses to challenge the impoverished portion of the client's model again [option (b) in (57)].

(79) **B:** *I couldn't hurt their feelings.*

The client responds with a Surface Structure which involves: (a) a modal operator of impossibility; (b) a very unspecified verb *hurt;* (c) a semantically ill-formed Cause-Effect, *I cause them to feel hurt,* relationship; (d) missing referential index on *feelings.*

(80) **T:**   *Does telling
someone no, or
that you feel
pushed around,
always hurt their
feelings?*

The therapist chooses to challenge the semantic ill-formedness of Cause-Effect relationship [option (c) in (79)], emphasizing the universality by inserting the universal quantifier *always*.

(81) **B:**   *Yes, nobody likes
to hear bad
things.*

The client verifies that the generalization is part of her model. In addition, her Surface Structure has violations: (a) missing referential index on *nobody*; (b) missing referential index on *things*; (c) a mind-reading violation, *nobody likes*; (d) a universal quantifier identifying a challengeable generalization — *nobody = all people not*; (e) a deletion associated with the Deep Structure predicate *bad — bad for whom?*

(82) **T:**   *Beth, can you
imagine that you
would like to
know if your
roommates feel
pushed around by
you so that you
could be more
sensitive to them?*

The therapist decides to continue to challenge the impoverishing generalization in the client's model. He asks the client to imagine an experience which contradicts the generalization she has in her model, or to verify or deny it.

(83) **B:**   *Yes.*

The client verifies it.

(84) **T:**   *Then, could you
also imagine your
roommates
wanting to know
when you feel
pushed around so
that they could
become more
sensitive to you?*

The therapist now uses the same situation which the client has just verified; this time, however, he uses it with the referential index shift.

| roommates | I (the client) |
| I (the client) | roommates |

(85) **B:**   *ummmmmmm
(pause) I guess*

The client hesitates, then verifies the fantasized situation. Her Sur-

you're right.	face Structure reply includes the deletion of a noun argument associated with *right*, i.e., *you're right about what?*
(86) **T:** *About what?*	The therapist asks for the deleted noun argument.
(87) **B:** *If I let them know when I feel pushed around or want something, then maybe they would be more sensitive.*	The client supplies the missing piece and acknowledges her understanding of how breaking her own generalization could be a good experience for her and her roommates.

The therapist at this point moved into some non-Meta-model techniques to give Beth a chance to integrate her new learnings and connect her new representations with her experience. This also allowed the therapist to see if there was anything else that interfered with Beth's communicating her needs to her roommates.

In this chapter, we have presented two transcripts which show therapists using the Meta-model techniques and only these techniques in the therapeutic encounter. Even with these artificial restrictions, the power of the Meta-model techniques is apparent. The Meta-model provides the therapist with a rich set of choices at each point in the therapeutic exchange. The overall effect of this results in an explicit direction or strategy for therapy — the enrichment and expansion of the limiting portions of the client's model. The Meta-model is not designed for use by itself, but rather as a tool to be integrated with the powerful techniques, verbal and non-verbal, available from the various forms of psychotherapy. We turn to this topic now.

FOOTNOTES FOR CHAPTER 5

1.   This is the same point that we have made before. Models, including the Meta-models we present here, are not claims about actually occurring events within the person, people and processes being modeled, but rather are explicit representations of the behavior of those things which allows one to see the rule-governed nature of the person, people, and processes being

modeled. Such models represent the portions of the process which are systematic. For example, in the Meta-model, there is no representation for the distance between the client and the Tower of London at different points in the session — we doubt that the client's behavior is systematic in this way. Some models may have as part of their purpose the representation of the inferred internal events in the person, people and processes being modeled — these are called simulation models.

2.   The word *they,* lacking referential indices in this sentence, may, in fact, refer back to the noun argument *women* in the previous Surface Structure. The noun argument *women* itself, however, also lacks a referential index.

3.   Experienced therapists will recognize patterns in the way a client responds or fails to respond to his or her context — in this case, specifically, the therapist. The client has failed consistently to respond to the therapist's questions. We are presently at work on an explicit model of therapeutic techniques for challenging these kinds of patterns — see *The Structure of Magic II* (forthcoming).

4.   The word *that* in the client's Surface Structure is missing a referential index — it may refer to the first clause *I'm a person, too.*

5.   Linguists refer to the verb *do* as a pro-verb. It functions for verbs in a manner parallel to the word *it* for nouns, and is as devoid of specific meaning as the pronoun *it.*

6.   The use of the referential index shift has proven in our experience to be particularly appropriate when the client is engaging in a great deal of mind-reading — the appropriate use of these more advanced techniques based on the verbal exchange will form part of the subject matter for *The Structure of Magic II.*

Chapter 6

ON BECOMING A
SORCERER'S APPRENTICE

The different forms of psychotherapy are all effective to some extent, although they look very different to most observers. The fact that these seemingly different approaches to the therapeutic encounter are all to some extent effective was a puzzle for some years. During these years both practitioners and theoreticians spent much energy and creativity arguing the necessary superiority of one form of psychotherapy over the others. In recent years, fortunately, this kind of debate has begun to disappear and psychotherapists from different schools have begun to show a lively interest in the methods and techniques of others. As Haley has commented, (*Advanced Techniques of Hypnosis & Therapy,* pp. 530-535)

> In the last decade, the idea of exploring new methods has been adopted by many psychiatrists and has led to such innovations as behavior therapy, conditioning treatment, and marital and family therapy. We have seen the passing of an emphasis upon ritual and a move toward judging therapeutic procedures by results instead of conformity to a particular school. It has even become respectable now to work in different ways with different types of patients . . . (Haley quoting Erickson directly) . . . "One of the important things to remember about technique . . . is your willingness to learn this technique and that technique and then to recognize that you, as an individual personality, are quite different from any of your teachers who taught you a particular technique. You need to extract from the

various techniques the particular elements that allow you to express yourself as a personality. The next most important thing about a technique is your awareness of the fact that every patient who comes in to you represents a different personality, a different attitude, a different background of experience. Your approach to him must be in terms of him as a person with a particular frame of reference for that day and the immediate situation."

People who come to us in therapy typically have pain in their lives and experience little or no choice in matters which they consider important. All therapies are confronted with the problem of responding adequately to such people. Responding adequately in this context means to us assisting in changing the client's experience in some way which enriches it. Rarely do therapies accomplish this by changing the world. Their approach, then, is typically to change the client's experience of the world. People do not operate directly on the world, but operate necessarily on the world through their perception or model of the world. Therapies, then, characteristically operate to change the client's model of the world and consequently the client's behavior and experiences.

Certain therapists, coming from dramatically different-appearing forms of psychotherapy, have come to be recognized as particularly effective in assisting clients in changing their experiences. Their behavior in psychotherapy appears to be extremely systematic to us in that they have a set of powerful techniques for directly challenging and expanding the client's model of the world. These techniques have been widely adopted by other therapists, but, unfortunately, without the dramatic results typical of this first group. The difference here seems to us to be that the first group of therapists have very clear intuitions about how to employ these techniques to challenge and expand the client's model. In other words, these psychotherapists are able to identify when the use of some particular technique is appropriate. The use of these same techniques by others often leads to very uneven results; sometimes they will succeed dramatically, other times they appear to miss altogether; at times the use of these techniques appears to be appropriate, at other times not.

We have thus far in this book presented a Meta-model for use by therapists in their verbal exchanges in the therapeutic encounter. The Meta-model is a tool that is available to therapists from any school of psychotherapy. Its practicality is two fold: first, it offers explicit direction (i.e., step-by-step and, therefore, learnable) for what to do next at any point in the therapeutic encounter, and second, anyone who is a native speaker of English already has the intuitions necessary to use the Meta-model and he only needs to become conscious of these intuitions.

As we have stated repeatedly, our Meta-model does not, by any means, exhaust the choices or possibilities of what a therapist might do in the therapeutic encounter. Rather, it is designed to be integrated with the techniques and methods in already established forms of psychotherapy. The integration of the explicit Meta-model with the techniques and methods of therapy in which you are already skilled will not only expand the choices you have as a therapist, but it will increase the potency of your style of therapy by making the interventions you use directed explicitly at expanding your client's model of the world. Thus, the Meta-model gives the therapist an explicit strategy for therapy.

We have two major goals in this final chapter:

1. We will select and present a number of these techniques from different forms of psychotherapy; in each case, we will demonstrate how these techniques implicitly challenge and expand the client's model. Thus, they share with the explicit Meta-model we have presented here the goal of operating directly on the client's representation of the world.

2. We will show how these techniques link up with the explicit steps in our Meta-model in a way which indicates when their use is appropriate.

The Second Ingredient: Reference Structures

One of the features of our experience which made it possible for us to develop an explicit Meta-model for the language of therapy was that each of us as native speakers of our language have consistent intuitions as to what are the full linguistic representations — the Deep Structures — of each sentence or Surface Structure we hear. As therapists, we can come to know exactly what is missing from the client's Surface Structure by comparing it to the Deep Structure from which we know it is derived. Thus, by asking for what is missing, we begin the process of recovering and expanding the client's model — the process of change.

We will call the Deep Structure the reference structure for the sentence, or Surface Structure, which we hear from our clients. It is the reference structure in the sense that the Deep Structure is the source from which the Surface Structure sentence is derived. The Deep Structure is the fullest linguistic representation of the world, but it is not the world itself. The Deep Structure itself is derived from a fuller and richer source. The reference structure for the Deep Structure is the sum total of all of the client's experiences of the world. The processes which specify what happens between the Deep Structure and the Surface Structure are the three universal processes of human modeling, the rules of representation themselves: Generalization, Deletion, and Distortion. These general processes have specific names and forms within the Meta-model which we have created with the concepts and mechanics suggested by the transformational model of language; for example, referential indices, deletion transformations and, semantic well-formedness conditions. These same three general processes of modeling determine the way that Deep Structures are derived from their source — the client's experience of the world. We suggest that the same set of specific concepts and mechanisms will continue to guide us in recovering the reference structure for the Deep Structure.[1]

The Meta-model for therapy that we have developed and presented here is, as we have stated repeatedly, a formal model. It is, specifically, formal in two senses of the word:

1. It is a model which is explicit — that is, it describes what the structure of the process of therapy is in a step-by-step manner.

2. It is a model which deals with form, not content. In other words, the Meta-model is neutral with respect to the content of the therapeutic encounter.

The first sense in which our Meta-model is formal guarantees that it is available to anyone willing to learn it — that is, since it is an explicit description of a process, it is learnable. The second sense in which the Meta-model is formal guarantees that it will have universal applicability[2] — no matter what the subject or content of the particular therapeutic session, the exchange between the therapist and the client will involve Surface Structures; these Surface Structures are the material on which the Meta-model is designed to operate.

Notice that, since the Meta-model is independent of content, there is nothing in it which would distinguish the Surface Structures produced by a client who was talking about his last trip to Arizona from the client who was talking about some intensely joyous or painful experience that he recently had with a close friend. This is the point at which the therapist's particular form of psychotherapy will indicate the content of the therapeutic session. For us, for example, when a person comes to us in therapy, we feel that they have come with some pain, some dissatisfaction about their present situation, and we generally begin by asking what they hope to gain by coming to us — that is, what they want.

Their reply, no matter what it is, (even, *I don't know*) is in the form of a Surface Structure, and we move into the process of therapy by then applying the Meta-model techniques. The initial question that we ask is not a question which we have shown to be demanded by the Meta-model. Rather, it is a question which we have developed out of our experiences in therapy — that is, our experiences in therapy have led us to understand that one of the necessary components of the therapeutic experience is for us to learn what it is that has brought the client to therapy.

The reference structure for the full linguistic representation of Deep Structure is the full range of human experience. As humans, we can be certain that each experience that we have will include certain elements or components. For the purpose of understanding these components of the reference structure for Deep Structure, we can divide them into two categories: the sensations which originate in the world, and the contribution which we make with our nervous systems to these sensations as we receive and process them, organizing them into the reference structure for the linguistic Deep Structures of our language. The exact nature of the sensations which arise in the world are not directly knowable as we use our nervous systems to model the world, even reaching out with our receptor systems, setting and calibrating them (the concept of forward feedback — Pribram, 1967), in accordance with the expectations which we derive from our present model of the world. The model which we create is, of course, subject to certain constraints imposed by the world — if my model is too divergent from the world, it will not serve me as an adequate guide for my behavior in the world. Again, the way that the model each of us develops will differ from the world is in the choices (normally, not conscious) which we make as we employ the three principles of modeling. This makes it possible for each of us to entertain a different model of the world and yet live in the same real world. Just as Deep Structures include certain necessary components, so, too, does the reference structure for Deep Structures. For example, we receive sensations through the five (minimally) senses of sight, hearing, touch, taste, and smell. Thus, one component of the reference structure for which we as therapists may check is whether the Deep Structures include descriptions of sensations arriving through each of these five senses — that is, does the full linguistic representation include descriptions which represent the client's ability to see, hear, touch, taste and smell. If one of these senses is not represented, then we may challenge the representation, requiring the client to re-connect the Deep Structure with its reference structure and to recover the deleted sensations, thus expanding and enriching the client's model.

While we have not yet developed an explicit structure for the range of human experience, we have some suggestions about what some of the necessary components of that reference structure will be. In addition to the check for the five senses, we have found it useful to employ a set of categories developed by Virginia Satir in her dynamic work in family systems and communication postures. Satir organizes the reference structure into three major components:

1. *The context* — what is happening in the world (i.e., in the client's representation of the world);
2. *The client's feelings* about what is happening in the world (as represented);
3. *The client's perceptions* of what others are feeling about what is happening in the world (as represented).

We are aware that, while the client's reports of feelings about what is happening will occur in the form of Surface Structures which are subject to the techniques of the Meta-model, we have not emphasized this as a necessary component of a well-formed Deep Structure. The client's feelings about what is happening in the world are, however, a necessary component of any well-formed reference structure. In other words, therapists may be sure that the reference structure is incomplete, or, in the terms we have developed in this book, not well formed, if the client's feelings are not represented in the reference structure. This is equivalent to saying that human emotions are a necessary component of human experience.

The point of mentioning this quite obvious fact is not to suggest that you, as a therapist, are not aware that people have feelings, but rather is the hope that you will recognize that, when you ask questions like, "How do you feel about that?" (whatever *that* might be) you are, in fact, asking your client for a fuller representation (than even Deep Structure) of your client's experience of the world. And what you are doing by asking this particular question is asking for what you know is a necessary component of the client's reference structure. This particular component of the reference structure is common to most therapies and is very useful information in our work as therapists. What is not common to most therapies and can make this question even more potent is that the client's answer will be a Surface Structure, subject to the well-formed-in-therapy conditions. This allows you to know more about your client's model, recovering one of the necessary components of the reference structure, and at the same time challenging and expanding the client's model. When this common question is seen from the point of view of the Meta-model, an additional and very potent question suggests itself. This new question, which is characteristic of Satir's work, is: "How do you feel about your feelings about what is happening?" Consider this question in the light of the Meta-model. This is essentially a request on the part of the therapist for the client to say how he feels about his reference structure — his model of the world — focusing specifically on his feelings about the image that he has of himself in his model. This, then, is an explicit way of directly approaching what is called in many therapies the client's self-esteem — a very potent area of the client's reference structure and one closely connected with the possibility of change for that person. The following sequence between a therapist and a client shows the way that the therapist gets to this aspect of the client's reference structure:

(1)	S:	*Paul just doesn't care about cleaning up the house.*	The client's Surface Structure claims that the client has knowledge about the inner state of another without stating how she gained this knowledge — mind-reading — thus violating the semantic well-formed-in-therapy conditions.
(2)	T:	*How do you know he doesn't care about it?*	The therapist chooses to challenge this semantic violation by asking the client to specify the process more fully.
(3)	S:	*He told me.*	The client supplies the information requested. Her Surface Structure, however, contains a deletion associated with the predicate *tell* — tell what?
(4)	T:	*He told you what, specifically?*	The therapist asks for the missing material.
(5)	S:	*He said, "I don't care about whether the house is clean or not."*	The client supplies the material.

(6) T: *How do you feel about his telling you he doesn't care about whether the house is clean or not?*

The therapist, using his knowledge that the client's reference structure must include her feelings about Paul's behavior as a necessary condition for being a well-formed-in-therapy reference structure, asks for that component.

(7) S: *I feel angry — in fact, damn mad . . . that's what we fight about all the time.*

The client supplies her feelings about Paul's behavior. Her new Surface Structure includes a universal quantifier *(all)* which identifies a generalization which the therapist may challenge.

(8) T: *How do you feel about feeling angry?*

The therapist ignores the violation of the well-formed-in-therapy condition concerning generalizations, and, instead, chooses to shift levels, asking the client about her feelings about her image of herself in her model of the world (her reference structure).

(9) S: *How do I feel about feeling angry?*

The client appears to be initially confused by the therapist's question requiring her to shift levels. This is a common reaction to such level shifts in our experience; clients, however, do have the resources to deal with this kind of maneuver.

(10) T: *Yes, how do you feel about feeling angry at Paul?*

The therapist repeats the question.

(11) S: *Well, I don't feel so good about it.*

The client supplies her feelings about her feelings — her self-esteem.

The therapist begins to explore the client's model at this new level by asking her to specify her verb more fully. Changes at this level — the level of self-esteem — are extremely important, since a person's self-image affects the way a person organizes his entire experience or reference structure. Therefore, changes at this level of structure permeate the client's entire model of the world.

These particular categories and techniques of Satir's offer a beginning to determine the set of the minimum necessary components for completeness of the well-formed-in-therapy reference structures. In observing extremely effective therapists, such as Satir, we have identified other types of categories which we offer as part of the set of minimum components which must be present for a reference structure to be well formed with respect to completeness, another way of checking for completeness in the client's reference structures. These include:

(a) The way the client is representing his past experiences in the present — these are often in the form of rules about his behavior;

(b) The way the client is representing his present experience in the present — that is, what the client is aware of now;

(c) The way the client is representing his possible future experiences in the present — that is, his expectations of what he expects the outcome of his behavior will be.

Notice that the four initial components presented by Satir (client's feelings, others' feelings, the context, client's feelings about his feelings) will occur as components of each of these three representations — the past, the present, and the future — as the client is representing them now. We have found these categories very useful in organizing our model and behavior in therapy in attempting to assist clients in developing complete reference structures. As you will have noticed in the explicit techniques of the Meta-model as presented in Chapters 3, 4, and 5, the Meta-model includes techniques for recovering and challenging the categories of the reference structure outlined here. Rules, based on the client's experience as represented in the present, are another name for generalizations based on the client's experience, as are the client's expectations. In each case, the client will present the material the therapist requests when challenging and enriching the client's model in the form of Surface Structures which are subject to the well-formed-in-therapy conditions which the Meta-model specifies. The point of presenting these categories is to offer some clear suggestions about what the necessary components of a complete, well-formed reference structure for the linguistic Deep Structure might be. Additional suggestions as to what the necessary components of a complete reference structure might be have been offered by various philosophers (any of the well-known western philosophers who dealt explicitly with epistomology — for example, in the empiricist tradition, Locke, Berkeley, Hume, and in the idealist tradition, Kant, Hegel, Vaihinger, etc.) and semanticists, logicians, linguists (for example, Korzybski, Humboldt, Carnap, Tarski, Chomsky, Katz, etc.).

For the remainder of this chapter we will select and discuss a number of techniques from different forms of psychotherapy. It is not our intention to teach these techniques here. Rather, in each case, we will show how the technique, as presently used, implicitly challenges the client's representation of the world, and how each of these techniques may be integrated with the Meta-model. We have selected these particular techniques simply because we are familiar with them and know from our experience that they are powerful therapeutic tools. We would also like to state that we are by no means saying they are any more powerful than other techniques, or that they lend themselves more readily to being integrated with the Meta-model, but rather we wish to provide a cross-section of techniques and chose from the ones we know.

Enactment: The Instant Re-Play of Experience

By *enactment* we refer to those techniques that involve the client in dramatizing an actual or fantasized experience. Enactment may involve only the client or it may involve other participants as well.

> By taking the word as an absolute, never investigating its personal significance, the word acquires a life of its own. Reifying the word in this way removes it from its practical function as a more or less efficient way of referring to a process which remains alive and has continually changing referents. Enactment is one way of keeping alive the words a person uses to characterize himself or someone else. Keeping his language connected to action permits feelings of change and growth. . . .
>
> (I. and M. Polster, *Gestalt Therapy Integration*, p. 00)

The solution (to the question of what the set of necessary components of a complete reference structure is) is complex. Fortunately for psychotherapy, this solution is not required for therapy to proceed. One way of avoiding this difficulty and at the same time gaining access to something closer to the client's reference structure is to have the client present the experiences from which the full linguistic representation was derived.[3] For example, the client has difficulty expressing anger toward her husband. We know this as she began by presenting a series of Surface Structures which we then subjected to the well-formed-in-therapy conditions, finally arriving at the full linguistic representation. At this point, in order to determine what the reference structure from which this full linguistic representation was derived is, we may ask the client to enact a specific occasion on which she was unable to express her anger at her husband. In addition to re-connecting the client's Deep Structures with a fuller approximation to their reference structures, the techniques of enactment typically accomplish two other things:

1. The client, in re-creating his experience, becomes aware of parts of the reference structure or experience which had no representation in the Deep Structure;
2. Enactment gives the therapist access to two important things:
   (a) A close approximation to the reference structure itself — the client's experience — and, therefore, provides the therapist with a wealth of accurate material to use in the therapeutic encounter;
   (b) The opportunity to see an example of modeling by the client directly. In other words, through enactment, the therapist has available an approximate reference structure. By comparing it with the client's verbal description of that experience, the therapist has an example of the generalizations, deletions and distortions typical of the client.

A number of things occur when the client enacts his experience. First, the client's present experience itself comes to challenge and expand his model of the world, as he experiences it in his enactment possibilities which had been previously deleted, and some of the missing portions of the representation are recovered. Secondly, the portions of the client's model which were vague and unfocused are clarified, as the enactment is a specific experience — equivalent to the supplying of referential indices by the client, in this case experientially rather than linguistically. The enactment is essentially a dramatization of what the client has represented as an event — the enactment itself denominalizes the representation; that is, it transforms the event back into a process, and, in this process, presents a much more fully specified image of the process (equivalent to more fully specifying the verb in Meta-model techniques). These four aspects of a typical enactment taken together result in an experience which lies in part outside the boundaries of the client's initial linguistic representation. Since the enactment technique implicitly challenges the client's model by these four aspects, if the enactment technique is integrated with the Meta-model techniques the result is that the enactment technique itself becomes more powerful and direct by explicitly challenging the client's linguistic representation.

In any therapeutic situation in which the technique of enactment is fully integrated with the Meta-model, the therapist has an extremely rich set of choices. Common to all of these is the suggestion that the therapist have the client describe his ongoing experience during the dramatization. This ongoing description, as well as any other verbal communications by the client to other participants in the enactment, will, of course, be a series of Surface Structures. The therapist subjects these Surface Structures to the well-formed-in-therapy conditions by using Meta-model questioning. This insures that the material which the enactment technique makes available *implicitly* is recovered in a completely *explicit* manner. The enactment technique is designed to make available a close approximation to the reference structure from which the impoverished portion of the client's linguistic representation was derived. The richer approximation to reference structure provided by enactment includes both verbal and analogical forms of communication. In addition to subjecting the client's reports of the ongoing experience, and his communications to other participants, to the well-formed-in-therapy conditions, the therapist has available this fuller representation — the enactment experience itself which the therapist may use as an approximate reference structure to compare directly with the client's verbal description.

The therapist may wish to use some of the necessary components of a complete reference structure suggested previously. The therapist may, for example, insure by questioning that the client is representing his feelings about the enactment experience explicitly by asking directly for those feelings. Or, for example, the therapist may pay particularly close attention to whether the client explicitly represents sensations gained through each of the five senses — that is, the therapist may check to see whether the client looks at and sees clearly the actions of the other participants in the dramatization, or the therapist may check to see whether the client listens and hears clearly the things said by himself and by the other participants in the dramatization.

Guided Fantasy — A Journey into the Unknown

By *guided fantasy* we refer to the process in which clients use their imagination to create a new experience for themselves.

Fantasy is an expansive force in a person's life — it reaches and stretches beyond the immediate people environment or event which may otherwise contain him. . . . Sometimes these extensions (fantasy) can gather such great force and poignancy that they achieve a presence which is more compelling than some real-life situations. . . . When these fantasies can emerge in the therapy experience, the renewal of energy may be vast, sometimes bordering on the unassimilable and often marking a new course in the individual's sense of self.

(Polster & Polster, *Gestalt Therapy Integrated*, 1973, p. 255.)

The purpose of guided fantasy is to create an experience for the client which, at least in part if not in its entirety, has not been previously represented in his model. Thus, guided fantasies are most appropriately used when the client's representation is too impoverished to offer an adequate number of choices for coping in this area. Most typically, these are cases where the client is either in a situation or feels that he will be in a situation in which he hasn't sufficient representation in his model to respond in a way that he thinks is adequate. Often, the client experiences a great deal of uncertainty and fear about the resolution of these situations. For example, a client feels blocked from expressing his feelings of softness and tenderness toward his son. He has never expressed these feelings and is very apprehensive about what will happen if he does, although he has no clear idea of what that happening might be. Here, we may choose to use a guided fantasy technique — having the client create by fantasy the experience which he both wants and fears. This experience will serve as a reference structure for the client, assisting him in overcoming his fear and ultimately giving him more choice in this area of his life. Guided fantasy, then, serves as a tool for the therapist in accomplishing two things:

1. It provides the client with an experience which is the basis for a representation in his model where previously there had been either no representation or inadequate representation. This provides him with a guide for future behavior and coping in this area;
2. It provides the therapist with an experience which the therapist can use to challenge the client's presently impoverished model.

In addition to these gains for both the therapist and the client, a guided fantasy is an opportunity for the therapist to observe the client creating not only a new experience but also a representation of that experience. Here, the therapist sees in the creation of this new fantasy experience the universal modeling processes of Generalization, Deletion and Distortion as they are typically employed by the client. The employment of the guided fantasy experience is parallel to the Meta-model technique of recovery of large-scale deletions under the category of modal operators. This technique differs from the process of enactment in that enactment recovers and brings into the present experience of the client something quite close to a reference structure from the client's *past*, while guided fantasy creates a reference structure for the client in the *present*.

Since guided fantasy is the creation of a reference structure, the therapist may wish to use the necessary components of a complete reference structure suggested previously in guiding the client's fantasy. Specifically, for example, the therapist may, by questioning, direct the client to report on his feelings at different points in the fantasy, or direct the client's attention to one or more of the five senses to insure a complete reference structure emerges in the client's fantasy.

We have found, in our experience, that guided fantasies often take the form of a metaphor rather than a direct representation of the "problem" that the client first identifies. For example, a client comes to a therapy session complaining that she is unable to get angry at someone with whom she works. Using the Meta-model techniques, we discover that the client also feels unable to express anger at her father and husband, and, in fact, she is unable to identify anyone at whom she feels she could express anger. There are a number of techniques available in the Meta-model to challenge this generalization; however, guided fantasy is particularly appropriate for situations in which the client has little or no representations in his model for such experiences. If, through the technique of guided fantasy, the client succeeds in expressing anger at someone in his fantasy (it doesn't matter whom), then he will have created a new reference structure which contradicts the generalization in his model. Often, once the client has successfully generated reference structures which contradict the generalization in his model, the generalization disappears, and the problems that were a result of the generalization also disappear or are reduced.

For example, once a young woman came into a seminar in which Meta-model techniques were being taught. Before the seminar began, she burst out into a frantic episode in which she claimed she was terrified that she was going crazy. Using Meta-model techniques, the teacher was able to determine that she felt she was losing control and did not know what was happening to her; her life was in turmoil, her future a frightening and dismal unknown. The teacher of the seminar asked her to close her eyes and tell him what she saw. After some initial difficulty, she proceeded to describe herself as standing on the edge of a large crevasse which was steep and foreboding. The teacher told her to slowly proceed into the crevasse and explore it, asking her to continually report on what she experienced, giving details of sight, hearing, feeling, smelling, and constantly reassuring her she could proceed through each obstacle. She finally proceeded down and back up, remarking, when she arrived at the top again, that it was still a gloomy day but that somehow she felt better. When she opened her eyes, her fear was gone and she felt that she could survive all that faced her. This experience offered a new reference structure in which this young woman was able to face an unknown experience; this new reference structure also expanded her model in such a way that it allowed her to believe that somehow she would survive whatever was happening to her in her life.

By the solution or resolution of a "problem" by metaphor in guided fantasy, we refer to a situation in which the client uses guided fantasy to create a new reference structure or experience in which he achieves that which was formerly not possible. Once the new situation — the one created in the fantasy — is successfully resolved, the "problem" which the client originally had either disappears or at least becomes less formidable, and, typically, the client feels able to cope with it. The created "problem" and the original "problem" must share a similarity of structure — they must both be "problems" relating to the same impoverishing generalization in the client's model of the world.[4]

Once a therapist has succeeded in developing a guided fantasy with his client, this fantasy, itself, is an experience available for the enactment process.

Therapeutic Double Binds

By *therapeutic double binds* we mean situations, imposed upon the client by the therapist, in which any response by the client will be an experience, or reference structure, which lies outside the client's model of the world. Thus, therapeutic double binds implicitly challenge the client's model by forcing him into an experience which contradicts the impoverishing limitations of his model. This experience then comes to serve as a reference structure which expands the client's model of the world. In the Meta-model, when the therapist uncovers an impoverishing generalization in the client's model, particularly one which involves a Cause-Effect, semantically ill-formed violation and/or a modal operator, the therapist may challenge this generalization by asking the client whether this generalization is necessarily or always true (see, Techniques for Challenging Generalizations, Chapter 4), to identify and dramatize an experience which contradicts this generalization (enactment), or, in a case in which the client does not have such an experience available, the therapist may ask the client to create an experience which contradicts his generalization (through the technique of guided fantasy). If these three techniques fail to produce the contradictory experience, or if the therapist is so inclined, he may choose to create a double-bind situation in which the client's response is an experience which contradicts the client's impoverishing generalization.

During one therapeutic session, in the course of using Meta-model techniques with a group, the therapist assisted the client in arriving at the generalization which was true in her model; namely, "I can't say *NO* to anyone because I can't hurt anyone's feelings." In this particular case, the therapist chose to use the Meta-model technique of asking what, specifically, would happen if the client were to say *NO* to someone. Her reply was that they would be badly hurt, that they might even die. Noticing the lack of a referential index of the noun argument *anyone*, the therapist decided to ask who, specifically, might be hurt and die. The client, now greatly agitated, recounted a traumatic experience from her childhood when she had said *NO* to her father's request to stay at home with him. Upon returning home later that same evening, the client discovered her father had died, and she had taken the responsibility for his death, attributing it to her having said *NO* to him.

The therapist now moved into an enactment technique, asking the client to recreate the situation described with her father. Even after the enactment technique showed that the original experience from which the client had made the generalization was one in which she had had no choice about whether she would stay with her father or not, she adamantly refused to give up her generalization. Here, although the enactment technique proved useful in recovering the traumatic experience, providing material which challenged certain other generalizations in the client's model, it did not, in itself, contradict the client's generalization about the consequences of saying *NO* to someone. In this case, note that the recovery and enactment of the original experience from which the client made a generalization did not contradict the generalization; it simply identified the source of the generalization. Thus, after the enactment, the client's model was still impoverished in this area — she still could not imagine saying *NO* to someone without there being unacceptable consequences. The therapist in this case next chose to use a therapeutic double-bind technique. What the therapist did was to tell the client to go around the room to each of the people in the group and say *NO* about something to each. The client reacted strongly, refusing to perform the task, making further statements such as

NO! It's impossible for me to say NO *to people!*

You can't expect me to do it just because you ask me to.

The client continued in this way for several minutes, refusing to carry out the task set for her by the therapist, until the therapist pointed out that she had, in fact, been saying *NO* to the therapist during this time! The therapist then pointed out that he had not been hurt and certainly had not died, contrary to her generalization. This experience was so powerful for the client that she was immediately able to move around the room and say *NO* to the other members of the group.

Consider the position in which the therapist placed the client by demanding that she say *NO* to the members of the group:

1. The client had stated her generalization
   I can't say NO *to anyone. ...*
2. The therapist structured a therapeutic double bind with the demand that the patient
   Say NO *to each of the people in this group.*
3. Notice the choices available to the client; she may
   (a) Say *NO* to each member of the group,
   or
   (b) Say *NO* to the therapist.
4. Whichever choice the client makes, she generates an experience which contradicts her original generalization. This experience serves the client as a reference structure to guide her in representing her world in richer terms.

The therapist makes the contradictory nature of the new experience explicit by pointing out (using the Meta-model technique) that the Cause-Effect relationship which the client's generalization claimed was necessarily true failed to be true in this experience.

One of the ways in which we have found therapeutic double binds particularly useful is in the area referred to by many therapies as homework. By homework we mean contracts which we make with the clients in which they agree to perform certain actions between therapeutic sessions. In the area of therapeutic double binds in homework, a client in a therapy session uncovered the generalization that

I can't try anything new because I might fail.

When the therapist, using Meta-model techniques, asked what

would happen if she did try something new and failed, she replied that she wasn't sure, but that it would be very bad. She expressed a great deal of fear of the consequences of failing at something new and again stated that it was impossible, therefore, for her to try something new. At this point, the therapist decided to impose a therapeutic double bind and use the time between sessions for carrying out this bind. He made a contract with her that she would, each day between this session and the next, try something new and fail at it. Again, notice the structure of the situation created by this demand by the therapist of the client:

1. The client has the generalization in her model
   I can't fail at anything new;
2. The therapist structures a double bind with the contract
   Each day, between this session and the next, you will try something new and fail at it;
3. Notice the choices available to the client:
   (a) She can try something new each day between this session and the next and fail at it, thus fulfilling the contract,

   or

   (b) She can fail to fulfill the contract, itself a new experience;
4. Whichever situation occurs, the client will have an experience which will contradict her generalization and give her a reference structure which increases the amount of her choices available in the world as represented in her model.

We are not suggesting that double binds constitute the only kind of homework, but rather that homework can consist of a double bind, and, further, that generalizations can be challenged by experiences extending after the interview or session itself. It is necessary only that these experiences create some new reference structure that contradicts the impoverishing portions of the client's model.

We would also like to state at this point that homework assignments also are useful for giving clients a direct chance to try out any new dimensions created in their models in the course of a therapeutic session.

Other Maps for the Same Territory

Human beings represent their experiences with systems other than language. The most basic distinction which has been offered as a way to understand the different maps that we, as humans, develop to guide ourselves in the world is the one between digital and analogical representational systems (see Bateson, 1973;

Wilden, 1973, for example). The best known digital representational system is the one which is the focus of our Meta-model — the natural language system. The most commonly referred to example of an analogical representational system is body expression. There are a number of therapies which deal primarily with these body or analogical representational systems. For example, therapies such as Rolfing, Bio-energetics, etc. challenge and expand the client's model by operating directly upon the client's analogical representation of the world of his experience. One point at which these two types of representational systems come together is in the use of voice quality — an analogical system — which is used to carry and express the primary digital system, natural language. One frequently cited example of a mixed system is that of dreams, wherein both digital and analogical representations are present.

For the purpose of therapy, it is essential for the therapist to understand that the full linguistic representation — the set of Deep Structures — is, itself, a derived model or representation of the world. Beyond the full linguistic representation is what we have referred to as the reference structure — that person's most complete representational system, the stored experiences that constitute that person's life history. This most complete model — the person's life experiences — is the reference structure not only for the set of Deep Structures which are the basis of the primary digital representational system, but also for those experiences which serve as the reference structures for the other human representational systems, analogical as well as digital.

One of the most powerful skills which we exercise as communicators and therapists is our ability to represent and communicate our experiences in any of the representational systems which we have available as humans. Further, experienced therapists will recognize the power of assisting clients in shifting their representational systems. For example, a client states that she has a severe headache. This is equivalent to the client's informing the therapist that she has represented some specific experience kinesthetically in a way which is causing her pain. One very powerful choice which the therapist has is to have her shift representational systems. Specifically, assuming that the therapist has already identified that the client has a highly developed ability to represent her experiences visually, the therapist tells the client to close her eyes and describe the specifics of the headache, at the same time forming a clearly focused image of the headache. There are variations of this which the therapist may employ to assist the client in achieving a visual representation. For example, he may have the client breathe deeply and, once a rhythm of breathing has been established, have the client exhale the headache forcefully onto a chair in front of her, creating a visual image there. The outcome of this shift of representational system is assisting the client in representing her experience in a representational system in which she will not cause herself pain. The power of the technique of shifting the client's experiences from one representational system to another can hardly be overestimated. In Volume II of *The Structure of Magic,* we present an explicit model for the identification and utilization of the client's most frequently employed representational system.

Congruity

Different portions of a person's reference structure can be expressed by different representational systems. These may occur simultaneously. There are two logical possibilities when two distinct representational systems are expressing different portions of the person's reference structure simultaneously.

First, the portion of the person's reference structure which one representational system is expressing fits with the portion of the person's reference structure which the other representational system is expressing. We refer to this situation as a consistent double message, or congruity or congruent communication by the person involved.

Secondly, the portion of the reference structure which one representational system is expressing does not fit with the portion of the reference structure which the other representational system is expressing. We refer to this situation as an inconsistent double message, incongruity or incongruent communication. For example, if, in a therapeutic session, the client is sitting calmly in a chair and speaking with a quiet, controlled voice, and states

I am really furious — God damn it, I'm not going to stand for this.

we have a classic example of an inconsistent double message or incongruent communication. The digital system (language) and an analogical system (body and voice quality) do not match.

One of the most impoverishing situations which we have encountered in therapy is the situation wherein a person maintains contradictory portions of his reference structure. Typically, these contradictory portions have the form of two contradictory generalizations which apply to the same area of behavior. Most frequently, the person whose reference structure includes these inconsistent generalizations has the experience of being immobilized, being profoundly confused, or oscillating between two inconsistent forms of behavior. This can be recognized by the therapist when he sees an incongruent or inconsistent double-message communication.

Notice that, in each of the techniques which we have presented in this chapter thus far, the overall strategy that the therapist has adopted is that specified explicitly by the Meta-model, to challenge and expand the impoverished portions of the client's model. Characteristically, this takes the form of either recovering (enactment) or creating (guided fantasy) therapeutic double binds, a reference structure which contradicts and, therefore, challenges the limiting generalizations in the client's model. In this case, the incongruent communication is, itself, an indicator of the two portions of a person's inconsistent reference structure, two generalizations which can serve as contradictory reference structures for each other. The therapist's strategy here is to bring the two contradictory generalizations into contact. This can be most directly accomplished by bringing these generalizations into the same representational system.

For example, during a therapeutic session, the therapist using Meta-model techniques assists a client in identifying a generalization in his model:

> *I should always appreciate my mother for all the things she did for me.*

Notice that from the Meta-model techniques alone this Surface Structure presents the therapist with a number of choices (the modal operator *should;* the universal quantifiers *always, all;* the lack of a referential index on the noun argument *things*). However, when the client was uttering this Surface Structure, the therapist observed that he had clenched his right fist and was gently pounding the arm of the chair in which he was sitting. This identifies an incongruent message. Ignoring for the time being the violations of the well-formed-in-therapy conditions in the client's Surface Structure, the therapist chooses to bring the incongruent pieces of the client's behavior into the same representational system. He does this by asking the client to express the analogical portion of the incongruent communication in the digital system. The client eventually responds with the Surface Structure:

> *I should always appreciate my mother for what she did for me, but she always sided with my father, and that pissed me off.*

Using Meta-model techniques, these two contradictory generalizations were kept in contact in the same representational system until the generalizations were challenged and the client arrived at a new model with more richness and detail — that he appreciated his mother for some actions and resented her for other actions.

One indication that the client's model is enriched is when there is *congruent* communication where there had previously been *incongruent* communication. This alignment of the person's separate representational systems which previously had been incongruent is a powerful experience for a client,[5] and is usually extremely noticeable to experienced therapists.

Family Therapy

By *family therapy* we refer to those therapies that conduct the therapeutic encounter with an entire family instead of an identified patient or client.

> All the above approaches are predicated on the necessity for viewing the symptoms of the identified patient or patients within the total family interaction, with the explicit theoretical belief that there is a relationship between the symptom of the identified patient and the total family interaction. The extent to which the therapist "believes" in family therapy will determine his emphasis on techniques that convey this orientation to the patient.
>
> (*Therapy, Comm. & Change*, p. 250)

The forms of family therapy with which we are most familiar make extensive use of the concept of congruity (Satir, Bateson, etc.). Here, congruent communication can be a useful tool for looking at individual members of the family or at the family as a unit. In fact, frequently recurring patterns of incongruent communication are claimed to be a major source of schizophrenia (see Jackson, 1967).

So far, we have focused exclusively on the Meta-model for therapy as a way to dictate an explicit strategy for individual therapy. We would now like briefly to raise the question of the relationship between our Meta-model and family therapy. Simply put, the overall strategy of the Meta-model is to identify, challenge and expand the impoverished and limiting portions of the individual's model of the world. One of the best indicators of an impoverished or limited portion of a person's model is an area of experience in which the person has pain or dissatisfaction. Similarly, in families, pain serves as a clear indication of impoverished and limited models of experience. In the context of family therapy, the same formal Meta-model principles apply. There is, however, at least one serious complication: a family system is more than a collection of the models of the individual members of that family. Specifically, in addition to the model of the world which each member has, the family has a shared model of themselves as a family and the way that they interact. Within their model, each family member has a model of the shared model of themselves as a part of the family unit. To get some idea of how complicated even a three-person family is, consider the following:

Suppose that we designate the family members by the letters *a, b,* and *c.* In this family system, there are the following perceptions or models (minimally):

a's model of himself;
b's model of herself;
c's model of himself;
a's model of himself and b together;
a's model of himself and c together;
a's model of b and c together;
a's model of himself with b and c together;
b's model of herself and a together;
b's model of herself and c together;
b's model of a and c together;
b's model of herself with a and c together;
c's model of himself and a together;
c's model of himself and b together;
c's model of a and b together;
c's model of himself with a and b together.

Issues of therapeutic strategy — whose model is it most useful to challenge and expand initially and how much, the degree of congruity of the models of the family system which each family member assumes he or she shares with the other family members — are all complications which do not arise in the context of individual therapy. We are presently working on an explicit, expanded Meta-model for family systems which takes these complications into consideration.

SUMMARY

In this chapter, we have presented a number of techniques from different, established forms of psychotherapy. Human beings have a number of representational systems, one of which is language. Each of these systems is derived from the sum total of the experiences which the individual has had — the reference structure. By recovering old, or creating new, reference structures, each of these techniques constitutes an implicit challenge to, and, therefore, an expansion and enrichment of, the client's model of the world. Furthermore, we have indicated how each of these tools may be integrated with the Meta-model techniques, resulting in an explicit strategy for therapy. One of our purposes has been to show how integration with the Meta-model techniques of the specific techniques of these different psychotherapies makes them more direct and, thus, more powerful. We invite you to imagine how the Meta-model tools could help you to improve, enlarge, and enrich the skills that you offer as a people-helper, thus beginning or assisting you on the road as a sorcerer's apprentice.

FOOTNOTES FOR CHAPTER 6

1. We intend to present a more complete and refined representation of reference structures and the specific mechanisms which map them into the various representational systems which humans use (e.g., the Deep Structures of language) in *The Structure of Magic II.*

2. The Meta-model we present is universal for therapy conducted in English. We are convinced that it can be easily adapted to other languages, as they are constructed on the same formal principles.

3. The enactment technique necessarily yields a representation closer to the reference source — the original experiences — than does the linguistic representation alone, as enactment involves linguistic representation plus other representational systems (e.g., the semantic/physical representational system). Here, the skill of the therapist in assisting the client in recalling and enacting the original experience is very important.

4. M. Erickson presents a clear case of this principle of solution by metaphor in *Advanced Techniques of Hypnosis and Therapy* (pp. 299-311).

5. This experience of alignment or congruity is part of the basis of the safeguard for the integrity of the client. As mentioned in Chapter 3, if the client deletes a portion of his Surface Structure or fails to assign a referential index to some element in his Surface Structure, the therapist has several choices. The therapist may have a strong intuition as to what the deleted portion of the Surface Structure is or what the identity of the missing referential index is. The therapist may choose to act on this intuition rather than to ask the client for the missing information. The safeguard for the client consists of the therapist's having the client say a Surface Structure which incorporates that intuition:

    C: *I'm scared.*

    T: *I want you to say this and pay attention to how you feel as you say it: "I'm scared of my father."*

The client then says the Surface Structure proposed by the therapist and pays attention to see whether he has an experience of alignment or an experience of congruity. If the result is congruent, the therapist's intuition is confirmed. If not, the therapist may use the Meta-model technique of asking for the missing material.

Conclusion

STRUCTURE OF THE FINAL INCANTATION OF BOOK I

It is not our purpose in this book to deny the magical quality of the therapeutic wizards whom we have experienced, but rather to show that magic, like other complex human activities, has structure and, given the resources, is, therefore, learnable. This book is one resource for a sorcerer's apprentice. This book, itself, like the magic it describes, has a structure.

Human beings live in a real world. We do not, however, operate directly or immediately upon that world, but rather we operate with a map or a series of maps which we use to guide our behavior. These maps, or representational systems, necessarily differ from the territory which they model by the three universal processes of human modeling: Generalization, Deletion, and Distortion. When people come to us in therapy expressing pain and dissatisfaction, the limitations that they experience are typically in their *representation* of the world, not in the world itself.

The most thoroughly studied and best understood of the representational systems of maps is human language. The most explicit and complete model of natural language is transformational grammar. Transformational grammar is, therefore, a Meta-model — a representation of the structure of human language — itself a representation of the world of experience.

Human language systems are themselves derived representations of a more complete model — the sum total of the experience the particular human being has had in his life. Transformational linguists have developed a number of concepts and mechanisms which describe how the way that people actually speak — their

Surface Structures — is derived from their full linguistic representation, the Deep Structures. The transformational Meta-model
describes these concepts and mechanisms explicitly; these are
specific cases of the general modeling processes of Generalization,
Distortion and Deletion.

Adapting the concepts and mechanisms of the transformational model of the human representational system of language for
the purposes of therapy, we developed a formal Meta-model for
therapy. The Meta-model is formal because:

(a) It is explicit; that is, it describes the process of therapy in a
step-by-step manner, guaranteeing that the Meta-model is
learnable. This results in an explicit strategy for therapy.

(b) It is independent of content, dealing with the form of the
process, and, therefore, has universal applicability.

The Meta-model relies only upon the intuitions which every native
speaker has of his language. The overall implication of the Meta-
model for therapy is the notion of *well formed in therapy*. This is
a set of conditions which must be met by the Surface Structures
which the client uses in therapy in order for these structures to be
acceptable. Using this appropriate grammar for therapy, we, as
therapists, can assist our clients in expanding the portions of their
representations which impoverish and limit them. This results in
enriching their lives in such a way that they experience more
options in their behavior, more opportunities to experience the
joys and richness that life has to offer. When integrated with the
people-helper skills which you already have available to you as a
therapist, this process of growth and change is profoundly ampli-
fied. This language of growth is then truly THE STRUCTURE OF
MAGIC.

We are delighted to point out not only that the last incanta-
tion for growth and potential is that you yourself can use this
language of growth to enrich the skills you have as a people-helper,
but also that you can use this language of growth to enrich your
own life and your *own* potential as a human being.

To be continued in *The Structure of Magic II*.

Table of Contents for
THE STRUCTURE OF MAGIC II

By John Grinder and Richard Bandler

Appendix A

A BRIEF OUTLINE OF
TRANSFORMATIONAL GRAMMAR

What we want to do in this appendix is to present a basic sketch of the structure of human language systems. This sketch is drawn from a formal theory of language known as transformational grammar and constitutes only the briefest outline of that theory.[1]

The theory of transformational grammar was developed to explicitly describe patterning in human language systems. You and I, as human beings, have consistent intuitions about the structure of our language and about its transformational grammar as a formal representation of those intuitions. For example, native speakers of English agree that the sequence of English words in (A) forms a sentence of their language while the sequence of words in (B) does not:

(A) *Hans' mother called Sigmund up.*
(B) *Called mother Sigmund Hans up.*

Furthermore, our intuitions are that the words *Hans* and *mother* go together in some way that the words *mother* and *called* do not. Again, when given sentence (C), a native speaker will recognize it as having a special relationship to (A).

(C) *Hans' mother called up Sigmund.*

which he will describe as *saying the same thing* or *having the same meaning.* Finally, a native speaker of English will identify (D) as a member of a special set of sentences

(D) *Murdering peasants can be dangerous.*

which constitutes the set of ambiguous sentences in English. These different classes of intuitions that you and I have, as native speakers of a natural language, can be described as:

1. Intuitions which allow me to consistently decide which sequences of words in my language constitute sentences (that is, well-formed sequences) of my language. We will refer to this as *well-formedness*.

2. Intuitions which allow me consistently to decide which words in a sentence go together to form a higher level unit or constituent. We will refer to this as *constituent structure.*

3. Intuitions which allow me consistently to decide which sentences have which kind of logical/semantic relations, relations such as, Which sentences of different structure or form have the same meaning? I will refer to this as *synonymy*. Relations such as, Which sentences have more than one meaning? we will refer to as *ambiguity*.

The grammar of a natural language is intended to represent these three classes of intuitions. The central data that a transformational grammar is designed to present in a systematic way are the intuitions native speakers such as you and I have about the structure of our language. By *consistently decide* we mean both that when we are presented with the same sentence at any two points in time our intuitions about its structure will be constant and also that other native speakers will have the same intuitions about the structure of that sentence. This behavior that we, as native speakers, exhibit is rule-governed behavior. That is to say that, although we may not be conscious of or able to articulate the rules that we use when we make intuitional judgments about the structure of our language, our behavior can be described by some set of explicit rules. Linguists construct grammars by developing these systems of rules. One of the things which such systems specify is which sequences of words in the language are well formed, that is, are sentences. This characteristic of rule systems addresses the first question, the membership question. In what follows, we distinguish between the *components* of the system and the *mechanics of the components* of that system. The major components of the system and the system itself do not involve concepts that are particularly difficult. We want to caution the reader not to become bogged down in the mechanics of the system, and for this reason we have separated them from the system proper.

WELL-FORMEDNESS AND CONSTITUENT STRUCTURE

One way of thinking about how grammars work, with respect to well-formedness, is to imagine the situation in which we have a large basket full of small slips of paper. Each slip of paper has a word of the English language written on it. Our friend, Atiko, is with me. Atiko is a member of á tribe called the Dasenetsch of South East Ethiopia. He does not speak or understand English. He draws out ten slips of paper at a time, arranging them from left to right in front of him in the order that he drew them from the basket. Now his task is to decide whether each sequence of ten words constitutes a well-formed sequence of English. We are able to assist him only by supplying him with a grammar or system of rules which he can use to decide whether the sequence is, in fact, well formed. Considered from this point of view, a grammar is a decision procedure which partitions the set of all possible sequences of English words into a set of well-formed sequences and a set of ill-formed sequences. Since Atiko does not know the English language, the rules must be explicit; the process that he uses cannot rely upon his intuitions to make judgments on any of the sequences. Further, if the system of rules constitutes an adequate grammar (with respect to well-formedness), then each member of the well-formed set will be judged well formed by native speakers of English and no member of the other set will be identified as well formed by native speakers. We will present the kind of rule systems used by transformational linguists shortly. These rule systems will be more intelligible if we first discuss constituent structure. Consider sentence (1) below.

(1) *Dick admitted Spiro had contacted the boys at ITT.*

Sentence (1) is judged by me, by you, and by all speakers of English to be well formed. Now, ask yourself whether you can detect any internal structure to the sentence. For example, do you find that the words *the* and *boys* go together in some intuitive way that the words *boys* and *at* do not? Or, again, do the words *had* and *contacted* go together in some way that *contacted* and *the* do not? For native speakers of English, the answer is *yes* for both of the questions. We can continue through the sentence, using our intuitions about the internal structure of the sentence to decide how to group the individual words in the sentence into higher level, multiple-word units. After we complete this first run through the sentence, we can begin again, this time grouping the initial groupings or constituents into higher level constituents. For example, the constituents *had contacted* and *the boys* go together in some way that *Spiro* and *had contacted* do not. This procedure is iterative. The intuitions of native speakers of English, like you and me, about the constituent structure of their language are consistent. To repeat, by consistent we mean that, given the same sentence now and again in ten years, our judgments about its internal structure will be constant. Furthermore, our judgments will match those of other native speakers of the language. Within the theory of transformational grammar, these kinds of intuitions are represented by what are called *tree structures*. There is a simple procedure for going from our intuitions to tree representation: words that go together in my intuitive groupings are dominated by (attached to) the same tree node. *The* and *boys* go together according to our intuitions about the initial groupings; therefore, the tree representation will include the structure

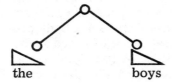

In actual tree representations, the nodes (here represented by O's) carry labels which identify their parts of speech, such as *S* for Sentence, *NP* for Noun Phrase, *VP* for Verb Phrase, *N* for Noun, *V* for Verb, *Det* for Determiner, *PP* for Prepositional Phrase, *Prep* for Preposition, etc. The actual representation for the constituent *the boys* looks like

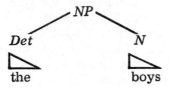

The tree (2) represents our intuitions about the internal structure of sentence (1): (See page 187)

Now, knowing the procedure for mapping onto tree representations from intuitions about grouping or constituent structure, you can read through the tree structures and see whether your intuitions match ours. For example, the words *had contacted the boys at ITT* form a constituent *(VP)*, but not *Spiro* and *had contacted*. This is reflected in the tree structure by the fact that the first sequence is exhaustively dominated (by exhaustively, we mean that the node that dominates these words dominates these words and no others) by a single node, but there is no single node

(2)

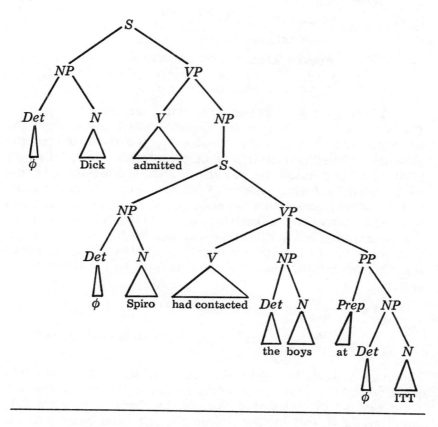

which exhaustively dominates the words *Spiro* and *had contacted*. We pointed out earlier that grammars are systems of rules. What, then, does the system of rules which specifies the tree structure (2) look like? In order to make the answer to this question more intelligible to you, we want to take a brief excursion into formal or logical systems.

Formal Systems
    Formal systems are composed of three components:[2]
        a vocabulary
        a set of axioms
        a set of rules of formation or derivation.
The more important concepts (for our purposes here) of formal systems can be illustrated by an extremely simple system — call it *SIMPLE*.[3] (See page 188)

System SIMPLE

vocabulary: $\underline{)}$, $\underline{(}$, $\underline{*}$

set of axioms: $\underline{*}$

rules of formation or derivation:

      (a) $* \longrightarrow) * ($

      (b) $* \longrightarrow \phi$

(The symbol ϕ represents the empty sequence.)
The symbol __ means that the material which appears on the left-hand side of it may be replaced by (be re-written as) the material on the right-hand side of the symbol. Now, let's turn SIMPLE on and watch the way it operates. The Meta-rule (a rule about rules) for formal systems of this class specifies that we must justify each statement that we make in the system. There are two possible justifications: either what we write down is an axiom of the system or it is a substitution specified by the rules of derivation from the line which we have just written. To begin, since there are no existing lines, the first line must be the axiom of the system

line	justification
*	axiom of the system

Now, we examine the line which we have just written and determine whether any of the symbols written there are on the left-hand side of the rules of derivation. The symbol $*$ is the only candidate, and, in fact, appears on the left hand of both of the rules of derivation for SIMPLE. We then choose one of the rules and write the next line

line	justification
*	axiom of the system
) * (	by rule of derivation (a)

We now repeat the procedure, scanning the last line and comparing the symbols there with the symbols which appear on the left hand of the rewrite arrows. Within this system, as long as we continue to choose rule of derivation (a), the procedure will continue.[4]

Suppose we choose the rule (a) twice more (See page 189)
When we examine the bottom line of the sequence, we find no symbols which occur on the left hand of a re-write arrow. The

line	justification
*	axiom of the system
) * (	by rule of derivation (a)
)) * ((	by rule of derivation (a)
))) * (((	by rule of derivation (a)

What happens now if we choose rule of derivation (b)?

line	justification
*	axiom of the system
) * (	by rule of derivation (a)
)) * ((	by rule of derivation (a)
))) * (((	by rule of derivation (a)
)))) ((((	by rule of derivation (b)

procedure now terminates. The results of the procedure, the collection of the lines top to bottom, is called the derivation. The final line of any such derivation is called a theorem of the system and is said to have been proven in the system. Finally, a sequence in the vocabulary of a system is said to be well formed if it is a theorem of that system. Looking at the system from an overall point of view, we can see that a sequence in the vocabulary of that system is well formed with respect to that system, just in case there is a derivation proceeding from an axiom of the system by means of the rules of derivation to a sequence which contains no symbol which occurs on the left-hand side of one of the rules of derivation for that system, a theorem. If we collect all of the theorems of a system, we have the set of well-formed sequences in the vocabulary of the system.

Now, we want to explicitly draw the parallelism between the system SIMPLE and natural language systems. The first task that we have when functioning as a linguist is to specify the set of well-formed sequences in the vocabulary of the natural language system for which we are attempting to construct a grammar. Using SIMPLE as a model, then, if we were able to specify a system of rules which gave as theorems for all the sequences of words in that language which native speakers judged to be well formed, then we would have succeeded in answering the membership question.

Some Mechanics of the Membership and Constituent Structure Issues

Let's see what a system of rules for natural language might be.

System DEEP

      Vocabulary: *S* (Sentence), *NP* (Noun Phrase), *VP* (Verb Phrase), *N* (Noun), *Det* (Determiner), *V* (Verb), *PP* (Prepositional Phrase), *Prep* (Preposition)

      Axiom: *S*

      Rules of derivation:

$$\text{(a)} \quad S \longrightarrow NP \quad VP$$

$$\text{(b)} \quad NP \longrightarrow \begin{Bmatrix} Det\ N & (PP) \\ S & \end{Bmatrix}$$

$$\text{(c)} \quad VP \longrightarrow V \quad (NP) \quad (PP)$$

$$\text{(d)} \quad PP \longrightarrow Prep \quad NP$$

$$NP \rightarrow \begin{Bmatrix} Det\ N & (PP) \\ S & \end{Bmatrix}$$

where symbols within parenthesis may be omitted and symbols within brackets represent a disjunctive choice, i.e., choose either one line of symbols or the other but not both.

    The Meta-rule for this system is the same as that mentioned for SIMPLE — each line of the derivation must either be an axiom or must be derivable from the previous line by a rule of derivation. Applying the procedure we used for SIMPLE, we have

line	justification
S	axiom of the system
NP VP	by rule of derivation a
Det N VP	by rule of derivation b
Det N V NP	by rule of derivation c
Det N V S	by rule of derivation b
Det N V NP VP	by rule of derivation a
Det N V Det N VP	by rule of derivation b
Det N V Det N V NP PP	by rule of derivation c
Det N V Det N V Det N PP	by rule of derivation b
Det N V Det N V Det N Prep NP	by rule of derivation d
Det N V Det N V Det N Prep Det N	by rule of derivation b

It is not difficult to map from derivations to tree representation; return to the first line of the derivation and begin reading down the derivation line by line. In each line, one rule of derivation was applied to replace one symbol by some other symbol (a). The rest of the symbols in the line have simply been carried down or re-copied from the line immediately above. These symbols carry no new information and are, therefore, redundant. We remove the redundancy by erasing or leaving out all of the symbols in each successive line of the derivation which are not affected by the rule of derivation which was applied. If we perform this operation for this first few lines of derivation, we have the figure

$$S$$

$$NP \qquad\qquad VP$$

$$Det \qquad\qquad N \qquad V \qquad\qquad NP$$

$$S$$

$$\cdot$$

$$\cdot$$

$$\cdot$$

$$\cdot$$

Now, we return to the first line of the derivation, and as we read down, we connect the symbol which was replaced in the upper line of each adjacent pair of lines with the symbol(s) which replaced it in the lower line of the pair. The results for the first few lines look like this:

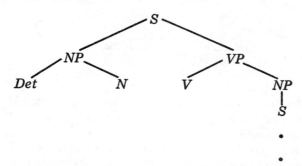

When we carry out these two procedures for the entire derivation, we have the tree representation

(3)

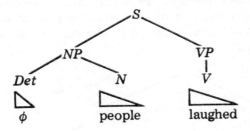

This tree structure is identical to tree structure **(2)** which we discussed earlier except that the words of English attached to the lowest nodes in tree **(2)** are missing from this tree. To apply these, we need a lexicon (or enlarged dictionary). This lexicon gives all of the words of English with certain additional information. For example, verbs are listed in this lexicon showing in what kind of tree structure they can be placed. The verb *admit* may fit into a tree structure under a *V* node if that *V* node is followed by an *NP* node,[5] as in tree structure **(2)**, but it cannot be placed in a tree structure under a *V* node if nothing follows that *V* node, as in

This kind of information listed in the lexicon prevents ill-formed sequences such as[6]

> *People admit
> **Dick laughed Spiro had contacted the boys at ITT*

For nouns, the lexicon gives information showing with what kinds of verbs the noun may be used. This information prevents ill-formed sequences such as[7]

The wall laughed
The wall admitted Spiro had contacted the boys at ITT
In general, then, the lexicon contains sufficient information to capture the dependencies between verbs and their accompanying noun phrases. Given the lexicon, we now need only a rule of substitution which checks the information in the lexicon against the tree structure and places the word involved under the lowest node if there is no conflict between the information in the lexicon and the structure of the tree. If we carry out this substitution operation for tree (3), one of the resulting trees will be tree (2), repeated here for convenience.

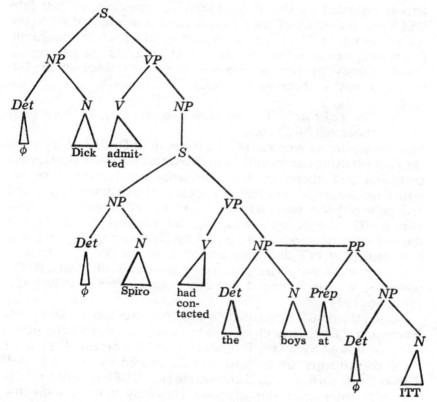

What, then, does the system DEEP do for us? First, DEEP represents intuitions about the constituent structure. How? Examine the rules of derivation for DEEP. Take rule (d), for example.

PP ⟶ Prep NP

In addition to being interpreted simply as a rule of derivation, rule

(d) can be interpreted as a rule of constituent structure; it makes the general claim that prepositional phrases (in English) are composed of a preposition followed by a noun phrase. More generally, each of the rules of derivation specifies that the symbols which appear on the right-hand side of the re-write arrow are the constituents which are exhaustively dominated by, and therefore replacements for, the symbol which appears on the left-hand side of the arrow. Secondly, the system DEEP is a first approximation for a system which represents intuitions about well-formedness; that is, what are the sentences of English. The answer provided by DEEP is all the theorems of DEEP. How do we decide whether the answer provided by DEEP is accurate? In principle, we just turn DEEP on, collect all of the theorems, and compare that set to the set of sentences identified by native speakers of the language. Practically, however, we can show that DEEP is not a complete answer simply by finding one well-formed sentence of English which is not a theorem of DEEP. Sentence (4) is one such sentence.

(4) *The boys at ITT were admitted by Dick to have been contacted by Spiro.*

How do we decide whether (4) is a theorem of DEEP? First, we go through (4) using our intuitions to determine what the appropriate groupings and, therefore, tree representations for them are. We notice on the initial grouping, for example, that the words *at* and *ITT* go together in some way that neither *boys* and *at* nor *ITT* and *were* do. On the second run through the sentence, we notice that the constituents *were admitted* and *by Dick* go together in a way that neither *at ITT* and *were admitted* nor *by Dick* and *to have been contacted* do. After proceeding systematically through the sentence, we can represent our intuitions by tree structure (5). (See page 195)

Our intuitions represented in this tree structure make several interesting claims. They claim that there is a constituent composed of *by*, followed by a *Det*, followed by an *N*, wherein all three of these constituents are exhaustively dominated by the node *NP*. This claim is sufficient to demonstrate that DEEP is only a partial answer to the membership question. How? By examining the rule of DEEP which specifies what constituents are exhaustively dominated by *NP*, that is, rule of derivation (b). Since no rule of derivation expands *NP* as by + *Det* + *N*, we see that in no derivation of DEEP (and, therefore, in no theorem of DEEP) can there be a case in which an *NP* directly dominates the element *by*. In order for that configuration to arise, there would have to have been a rule for the form. We, therefore, can conclude that there is

(5)

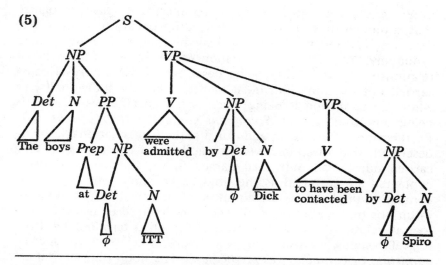

at least one well-formed sequence of English which DEEP fails to enumerate. But before we try to find a way to supplement DEEP with an additional system or some additional rules of derivation, we want to talk about our intuition about synonymy.

SYNONYMY

Check your intuitions about the relationship between sentence (2) and sentence (4), repeated below.

(2) *Dick admitted Spiro had contacted the boys at ITT.*

(4) *The boys at ITT were admitted by Dick to have been contacted by Spiro.*

Native speakers of English judge the sentences (2) and (4) to be synonymous. Synonymy is a relationship which holds between two (or more) sentences when they always have the same truth value — they are always both true or always both false. In other words, assume that the words *Dick* and *Spiro* and *the boys at ITT* refer to the same things as they are used in both sentences (2) and (4). Can you imagine a world, logically consistent, in which one of these sentences is true and the other false? If you are unable to, then the pair is said to be synonymous.[8] So, not only does sentence (4) represent a counter example to the claim that DEEP is an adequate grammar with respect to well-formedness, but it — along with sentence (2) — brings up the issue of how intuitions of synonymy are to be represented, how to determine which sentences of different form or structure have the same meaning. In other words, you and I, as native speakers of English, recognize that, although they are of a radically different form or structure, sentences (2) and (4) have a special meaning relationship called synonymy. In both of the sentences, there is an activity or relationship of *admitting* being described. This activity is being carried out by some individual named Dick; the individual(s) to whom an admission is being made is not specified, and what is being admitted is that *Spiro had contacted the boys at ITT*. Furthermore, there is an additional activity or relationship being described, that of *contacting*. This activity of contacting is being carried out by an individual named Spiro, the person(s) being contacted are specified as the boys at ITT, and what Spiro was contacting the boys at ITT about is left unspecified. The kind of intuitions that we are describing now are referred to as meaning or logical relationships. Again borrowing some terminology from logical systems, we will refer to activities or relationships such as *admitting* or *contacting* as *predicates*.[9] The noun phrases that are associated with these relationships or predicates we will call *the arguments of the predicate*. Using these terms, we can characterize the meaning relations in sentences (2) and (4). The major meaning relationship or predicate in these synonymous sentences is *admit*. The predicate *admit* has three arguments, the individual making the admission (i.e., Dick), the individual to whom the admission is being made (not specified), and the thing that is being admitted (Spiro had contacted the boys at ITT). We can represent these intuitions using a form from logical systems,

(6) admit^3 (Dick, _____, Spiro had contacted the boys at ITT)

where the super-script 3 on the predicate specifies the number of arguments associated with that predicate, and the blank space indicates a missing argument. The third of these arguments is complex, itself being composed of a predicate with its arguments.

(7) contact^3 (Spiro, the boys at ITT, _____)

The unspecified argument of the predicate *contact* is the argument which specifies what it was that the boys at ITT were contacted by Spiro about. We can combine the information in (6) and (7) into a single form

(8) admit^3 (Dick, _____, (contact^3 [Spiro, the boys at ITT, _____]))

These meaning relationships are represented in the theory of transformational grammar at the level of the theorems of DEEP. If you examine sentence (2), you will notice that, except for the arguments that are missing altogether, the logical or meaning relations are expressed directly. For example, the predicates and their arguments are located contiguously, and the grammatical relations (such as subject of the verb [the first noun phrase to the left of the verb] and logical relations [such as which argument is in first position]) are parallel. The subject of the verb *admit* and the first argument of the predicate is the same noun phrase *Dick.* Notice that the fact that the grammatical relations and the logical relations parallel each other and the fact that sentences (2) and (4) are synonymous could be represented if there were some way of deriving both (2) and (4) from the same structure. This, in fact, is the function that transformations have in grammatical systems.

The Transformational Component

On the basis of what we have already said, there are at least two difficulties that transformations must resolve: the transformational system must represent intuitions about the well-formedness of sentences such as (4), not represented by DEEP, and transformations must represent the intuition that you and I have that the two sentences (2) and (4) mean the same thing, the relationship of synonymy. Both of these objectives can be accomplished by having transformations from the system DEEP and then having transformations derive all of the sentences of the language as the theorems of that system from the theorems of DEEP. The derivation of synonymous sentences is then effected in this way: two (or more) sentences will be considered synonymous just in case they are derived from the same axiom. We want to take a closer look at the transformational system.

The Mechanics of the Transformational Component

The transformational system looks like

System/TRANS

Vocabulary: The vocabulary of system DEEP plus variable names X, Y, Z, etc.

Axioms: The theorems of the system DEEP.

Rules of derivation: The transformations of English.

In DEEP, the rules of derivation were of the form

$$A \longrightarrow BCD$$

that is, some symbol is replaced by some other symbol(s). In TRANS, the rules of derivation are somewhat different. Each consists of two parts: the *structural index* and the *structural change*. The purpose of the structural index is to identify the structure of the tree representations which are to be transformed or operated upon. We take the PASSIVE transformation as an example. The structural index for the PASSIVE transformation is:

$$X \; NP^1 \; V \; NP^2 \; Y$$

We read this formula as follows: the structural index of the PASSIVE transformation picks out any tree structure which has the following form: Any sequence of nodes (covered by the variable name *X*), followed by a noun phrase (identified as *NP1*), followed by a verb, followed by another noun phrase (identified as *NP2*). This formula of labeled nodes identifies a whole class of tree representations with the structure specified by the formula, tree representations that are as follows:

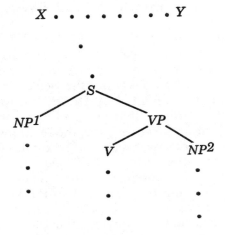

Once the appropriate tree representations are picked out by the structural index, then they may be transformed or mapped into a new tree structure. The purpose of the second part, the structural change, is to specify what changes are to be made to the input tree; that is, the structural change specifies the structure of the output tree. The structural change for the PASSIVE transformation is:

$$X \quad NP2 \quad be \ + \ V \ + \ en \quad by \ + \ NP1 \quad Y$$

The structural change of a transformation can be interpreted as instruction for how we are to change the input tree in order to get the right output tree. Specifically, the structural change for the PASSIVE transformation specifies that the structure of the output tree will be all the same nodes which were originally covered by the variable *X*, followed by the noun phrase which in the input tree was to the right of the verb *(NP2)*, followed by the element *be*, followed by the verb, followed by the element *en*, followed by the element *by*, followed by the noun phrase which originally appeared to the left of the verb *(NP¹)*. So, in tree form, the output of the transformation looks like

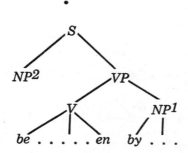

In more general terms, then, the effect of the PASSIVE transformation is, first of all, to permute or alter the order of the two *NP*s identified in the structural index, and secondly, to add some new elements.[10] To show the similarity between this kind of rule of derivation and that of the system DEEP, note that we can present this transformation in the same format as the one that we used for the rules of derivation of DEEP[11]

$$X\ NP^1\ V\ NP^2\ Y \longrightarrow X\ NP^2\ \text{be} + V + \text{en by} + NP^1\ Y$$

where the material which appears on the left-hand side of the arrow is the structural index and the material which appears on the right-hand side of the arrow is the structural change. I want to point out several differences between the two types of rules: the rules of DEEP accept as input and give as output linear sequences of symbols, while the rules of TRANS accept as input and give as output hierarchically arranged tree structures. The rules of DEEP are stated in a vocabulary which does not include variables, while those of TRANS use variables extensively, and finally, the rules of TRANS have the power to change more than one symbol at a time while those of DEEP do not. In general, the rules of TRANS are much more powerful than the rules of DEEP. Using the tree representations, I show the effect of the transformation PASSIVE (see page 200).

In the grammar of English, linguists have been able to identify a number of transformations. At this point in the presentation of

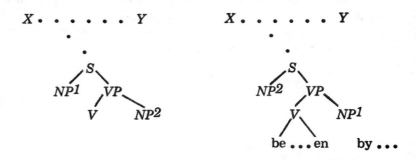

the system, I want to mention only one additional transformation — RAISING.

$$X \quad V \quad [\underset{S}{NP} \quad \underset{S}{Y}] \quad Z \longrightarrow X \quad V \quad NP \quad [\underset{S}{Y}] \quad \underset{S}{Z}$$

The overall derivation has the same effect as any derivation in a formal system: it carries the axioms of the system by the rules of derivation into the theorems or well-formed sequences (and, in this case, tree structures) of the system. If you compare the theorem for which we have just given the derivation with the tree representation (4), you will discover that, except for a few node differences which are affected by some minor clean-up transformations of English, the two trees are identical. Now, how does this account for the intuitions of well-formedness and synonymy? First, we showed that the system DEEP failed to account for at least one well-formed sentence of English, namely, sentence (4). Notice now that DEEP plus TRANS, in fact, accounts for that sentence. In order for us to explain how the synonymy question is handled, we need to develop some terminology.

The Complete Model

Within the theory of transformational grammar, each sentence receives a double analysis: an analysis of the constituent structure, or what things go together, and an analysis of the meaning, or logical relations. Transformational grammar makes the claim that, in order to capture the consistent intuitions that you and I have as native speakers of English, two distinct levels of structure must be identified. These are called the Deep Structure and the Surface Structure. The Deep Structure is the level of structure in which the meaning or logical relations information is stated for the sentence under analysis; the Surface Structure is the level of

(a)

line

justification
axiom of the system
(theorem of DEEP)

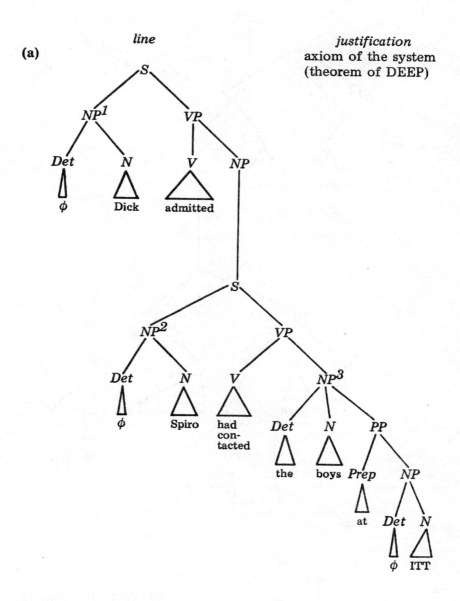

by rule of derivation (a)

(b)

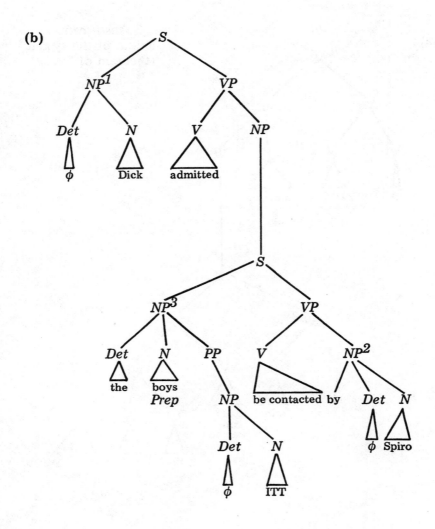

by rule of derivation (a)

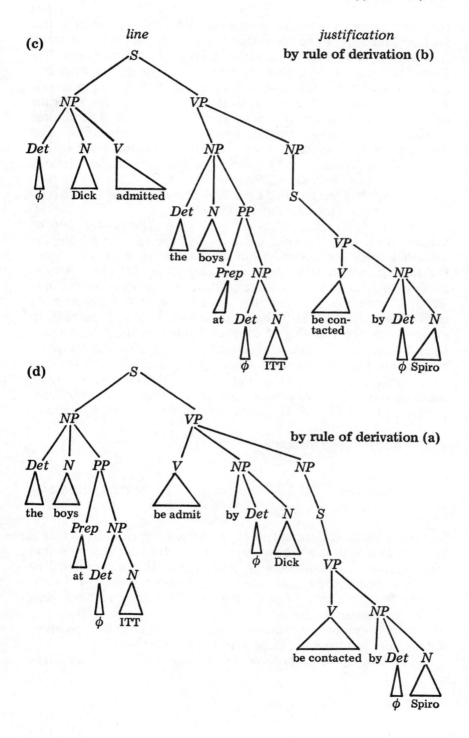

structure in which constituent structure information is stated. The Surface Structure is the form that the sentence actually has when it is used by you and me as native speakers of the language. The Deep Structure never appears directly in the use of the language, although you and I have consistent intuitions about the relations which hold between the elements of the Deep Structure. In terms of the systems that we have been presenting, the Deep Structures of English are the set of theorems for the system DEEP. The theorems of TRANS are the set of Surface Structures of English.

> *Deep Structures of English* — meaning or logical relations (theorems of DEEP)
>
> *Surface Structures of English* — constituents structure relations (theorems of TRANS)

Now for the relationship of synonymy. The relationship of synonymy is said to hold between two Surface Structures of English if they are derived from the same Deep Structure. Since the point at which meaning relations are stated for the sentences of English is at the level of Deep Structure, the transformations which change the form of that sentence as it goes through its derivation to Surface Structure add no dimensions of meaning. In other words, the meaning of a sentence is independent of the post Deep Structure form that it receives by the transformations which map it into Surface Structure. Another way of stating this result is to say that two theorems of the system TRANS have the same meaning (i.e., are synonymous) just in case they are derived from the same axiom. Figure (10) shows this relation of synonymy.

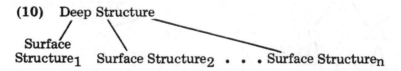

(10)   Deep Structure

Surface
Structure$_1$ Surface Structure$_2$ . . . Surface Structure$_n$

So each Surface Structure derived from the same Deep Structure is synonymous with every other Surface Structure derived from that same source. Take sentences (2) and (4), which are synonymous:

(2) *Dick admitted Spiro had contacted the boys at ITT.*

(4) *The boys at ITT were admitted by Dick to have been contacted by Spiro.*

There are a number of additional sentences which are theorems of TRANS derived from the same axiom. For example:

(11) *That Spiro had contacted the boys at ITT was admitted by Dick.*

(12) *Dick admitted to someone that Spiro had contacted the boys at ITT about something.*

If you examine sentence (11) carefully, you will see that it is the result of a derivation from the same Deep Structure which includes only one application of the rules of derivation (a), that is, the PASSIVE transformation. Sentence (12) is more important. Remember the discussion of the kind of information which the lexicon contains regarding verbs; specifically, we characterized the verb *admit* as a three-place predicate.

    admit^3 (person admitting, person being admitted to, thing admitted)

In sentence (2), which we have been calling the theorem of DEEP, the counter argument is missing.

    admit^3 (Dick,＿＿＿＿, Spiro had contacted the boys at ITT)

Now we can correct an earlier simplification. The actual theorem of DEEP, the Deep Structure underlying (2), (4), and (11), is the tree structure for (12), in which all of the arguments of the predicate *admit* have a representation. The tree structure looks like the following (see page 206).

    Since sentence (2) and sentence (12) are synonymous, the system TRANS must derive them from the same theorem. The Surface Structure sentence (12) is virtually identical with its Deep Structure.[12] Two noun phrase arguments are missing from the Surface Structure (2). This fact uncovers for us a distinct and extremely important class of transformations of English. The transformations that we have presented up to this point have had the effect of permuting or changing the order of noun phrase arguments in the tree structure; these are referred to as Permutation transformations. The transformations involved in the derivation of sentence (2) in the system TRANS have, as their effect, the removal of constituents from the tree structure; these constitute the class of Deletion transformations. The specific transformation which is involved in the derivation of (2) is called *Unspecified NP Deletion.* It was applied twice in the derivation of (2) to remove the two constituents *to someone* and *about something.* The existence of this transformation, then, allows us to understand the relationship, that is, the derivation, between axiom (12) and theorem (2).

    What we have presented so far is the representation of the consistent intuitions about language for which any adequate grammar of a natural language system must provide. Figure (13) may help you to visualize the entire system (see page 207).

    Further, it is at the level of Deep Structure that the meaning of logical relations is stated, while it is at the level of Surface

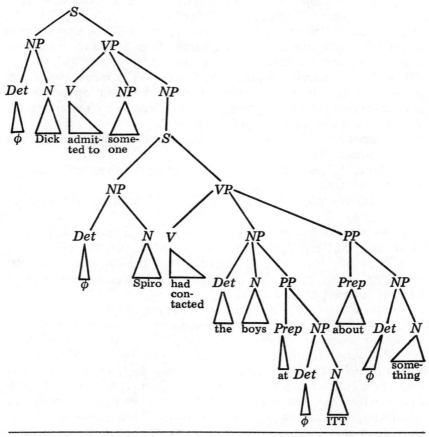

Structure that the constituent structure relations are stated. The set of well-formed membership question sentences in the language is the set of all theorems of TRANS. The intuition of synonymy is answered as every Surface Structure derived from the same Deep Structure is synonymous with every other Surface Structure derived from that Deep Structure.

The last of the three intuitions can now be represented, *ambiguity*. Ambiguity refers to the experience native speakers have when they understand a sentence to have more than one distinct meaning. Sentence **(14)** is the example of an ambiguous sentence which we presented earlier.

(14) *Murdering peasants can be dangerous.*

Our intuitions about this sentence are that it can be understood to mean either that peasants who murder can be dangerous or that for someone to murder peasants can be dangerous. If we represent

(13)

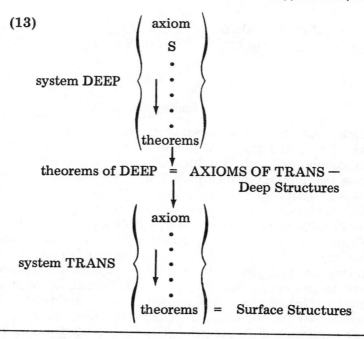

theorems of DEEP = AXIOMS OF TRANS —
Deep Structures

these two distinct meanings by the symbols *A* and *B*, then how can we account for this property of ambiguity within the system of transformational grammar that we have developed here? The answer is quite simple: consider the case of synonymy. Synonymy is the case in which the same Deep Structure maps onto more than one Surface Structure. Ambiguity is the inverse of synonymy, namely, where different Deep Structures map onto the same Surface Structures. In other words, a Surface Structure will be ambiguous if there is more than one derivation leading from distinct Deep Structures. If there are two such derivations, then the Surface Structure which results is ambiguous in two ways, that is, it is connected by derivations with two distinct Deep Structures. If there are *n* such derivations, then the resulting Surface Structure is *n* ways ambiguous. Figure (15) may help you to see the relationship of ambiguity in transformational terms (see page 208).

This last characterization of the relationship of ambiguity in transformational terms completes the sketch of the theory of transformational grammar which we want to present in this work.

Transformational grammar is the name of the portion of the field of linguistic research which we have used as a reference point in adapting linguistic models as a Meta-model for therapy. At this point in time in the development of the field of transformational

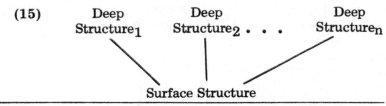

(15)

Deep
Structure$_1$

Deep
Structure$_2$ . . .

Deep
Structure$_n$

Surface Structure

grammar, there are at least two groups of researchers who consider themselves and members of the other group to have a distinctive and competing model for the dominant paradigm in linguistics. These two groups call their models the Extended Standard Theory and the Generative Semantics models. The concepts and processes which we have selected from transformational grammar are available in both models. In other words, both groups of people will be able to identify the formally equivalent concepts and processes in their model. Models are useful for much that falls outside formal equivalence. Specifically, the names of the concepts and processes given to the experiences of having intuitions about language present different images. They suggest through mechanisms such as presuppositions, entailments, invited inferences, and the syntax of their expression different perceptions and attitudes. The majority of the names we have chosen to use here are drawn from the Extended Standard Theory. For the purposes of perceiving language while doing linguistics analysis and for formal elegance, we chose the Generative Semantics model. For the purposes of describing our experiences in therapy, in talking to people training themselves to be therapists, we have found the terminology of the Extended Standard Theory more useful; thus, it was our choice in this book. We have attempted in the Glossary to give the notational equivalences in the Generative Semantics model for the terms used here in the cases which seem important to us. We have an intuition that the Generative Semantics model will be most useful in the area of Logical Semantic relations. Some fine work is being done in that area by linguists George Lakoff, Lauri Kartunnen, Georgia Green, Jerry Morgan, Larry Horne, Paul Postal, Haj Ross, Mass-aki Yamanashi, Dave Dowty, etc.; by logicians Hans Herzberger, Bas van Fraasen, Saul Kripke, etc.; and by people in Artificial Intelligence such as Roger Schank, Terry Winograd, etc. These kinds of images have been useful to both of us in representing and communicating our experiences in therapy.

FOOTNOTES FOR APPENDIX A

1. For a fuller presentation of the theory of transformational grammar, see Chomsky (1957), (1965); Grinder and Elgin (1973); Langacker (1973); etc.

2. For a fuller discussion, see any introductory logic text; for example, Tarsky (1943), Kripke (1972).

3. Because it is.

4. Since there is no limit to the number of times that we may choose rule of derivation (a), there is no longer sequence of lines, and, therefore, the set of lines generated is infinite. Actually, if you examine the structure of the set of rules of derivation, you'll find that the axiom expands into itself; that is, the symbol ± appears on both sides of the re-write arrow. The symbol, therefore, is constantly replacing itself. This property of rule system is called recursion; it guarantees that the set will generate an infinite set of lines of derivation.

5. This is actually incomplete as the verb *admit* goes into a tree structure in which the verb is followed by two *NP* nodes; we will correct this later.

6. What is going on in the sentences listed is that the structural requirements of the verbs involved are being violated. For example, the verb *laugh* requires that it not be followed by some noun phrase. In more traditional grammatical terms, the verb *laugh* is an intransitive verb; it takes no direct object.

7. What is going on in the sentences listed is that the meaning requirements, or the selectional restrictions of the verbs, are being violated. Verbs such as *laugh* and *admit* require that their subjects be human (or, at least, animate).

8. If you are able to, phone us and charge it to the publisher.

9. See any introductory treatment of the predicate calculas; for example, in the sources listed in Footnote 6.

10. Notice that the transformation itself created the constituent structure which we could not account for by the rules of derivation for DEEP. Specifically, the sub-tree

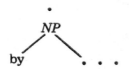

11. The similarities and differences in different classes of rules are studied in Automata Theory, and the results of this field have been extremely important in linguistics, both in evaluating older models of language structure and in developing new models. See, for example, T. L. Booth's *Sequential Machines and Automata Theory* (John Wiley and Sons, Inc., 1967). For comments on the relationship and importance of results in this field to the field of linguistics, see Chomsky, and G. A. Miller (1958, 1963), Chomsky (1959a, 1959b, 1963).

12. Once again, we are simplifying here; for example, the PP *at ITT* in a more complete analysis would be identified as itself being derived from an entire sentence in Deep Structure.

Appendix B

SYNTACTIC ENVIRONMENTS FOR IDENTIFYING NATURAL LANGUAGE PRESUPPOSITIONS IN ENGLISH

Our purpose in presenting the material in this appendix is to indicate the scope and complexity of the natural language phenomenon of presuppositions. In addition, by listing some of the more common syntactic environments in which presuppositions occur we provide an opportunity to practice for those students who are interested in sharpening their intuitions in recognizing presuppositions. The list of syntactic environments is not exhaustive, and we will not attempt to present any of the theories which have been proposed by different linguists, logicians, semanticists, or philosophers to account for presuppositions. Rather, our objective is more practical.

At the present time, presuppositions are a major focus of study for a number of linguists, especially linguists who consider themselves Generative Semanticists. In compiling this list of syntactic environments, we have borrowed heavily from the work of Lauri Kartunnen. See the Bibliography for sources.

1. **Simple Presuppositions.**
   These are syntactic environments in which the existence of some entity is required for the sentence to make sense (to be either true or false).
   (a) **Proper Names.**
       (*George Smith* left the party early.)———➤(There exists someone named George Smith) where———➤ means presupposes

(b) **Pronouns.** *Her, him, they*
  (I saw *him* leave.)————▶(There exists some male [i.e., him])

(c) **Definite Descriptions.**
  (I liked *the woman with the silver earrings.*)————▶ (There exists a woman with silver earrings.)

(d) **Generic Noun Phrases.**
  Noun arguments standing for a whole class. (If *wombats* have no trees to climb in, they are sad.) (There are wombats.)

(e) **Some Quantifiers.** *All, each, every, some, many, few, none*
  (If *some of the dragons* show up, I'm leaving.) ————▶(There are dragons.)

2. **Complex Presuppositions.**
Cases in which more than the simple existence of an element is presupposed.

  (a) **Relative Clauses.**
  Complex noun arguments, with a noun followed by a phrase beginning with *who, which,* or *that.* (*Several of the women who had spoken to you* left the shop.)————▶(Several women had spoken to you.)

  (b) **Subordinate Clauses of Time.**
  Clauses identified by the cue words *before, after, during, as, since, prior, when, while* (If the judge was home *when I stopped by her house,* she didn't answer her door.)————▶(I stopped by the judge's house.)

  (c) **Cleft Sentence.**
  Sentences beginning with It $\begin{Bmatrix} was \\ is \end{Bmatrix}$ noun argument, (It was the extra pressure which shattered the window.)————▶(Something shattered the window.)

  (d) **Psuedo-Cleft Sentences.**
  Identified by the form, *What* [Sentence] *is* [sentence] (What Sharon hopes to do is to become well liked.)————▶(Sharon hopes to do something.)

  (e) **Stressed Sentences.**
  Voice stress (If Margaret has talked to THE POLICE, we're finished.)————▶(Margaret has talked to someone.)

(f)   **Complex Adjectives.** *New, old, former, present, previous*
(If Fredo wears his new ring, I'll be blown away.)
———→(Fredo had/has an old ring.)

(g)   **Ordinal Numerals.** *First, second, third, fourth, another*
(If you can find a third clue in this letter, I'll make
you a mosquito pie.)———→(There are two clues
already found.)

(h)   **Comparatives.** *-er, more, less*
(If you know bett*er* riders than Sue does, tell me
who they are.)———→(Sue knows [at least] one
rider.) (If you know bett*er* riders than Sue is, tell
me who they are.)———→(Sue is a rider.)

(i)   **Comparative As.** *As x as . . .*
(If her daughter is *as funny as* her husband is, we'll
all enjoy ourselves.)———→(Her husband is funny.)

(j)   **Repetitive Cue Words.** *Too, also, either, again, back*
(If she tells me that *again*, I'll kiss her.)———→(She
has told me that before.)

(k)   **Repetitive Verbs and Adverbs.**
Verbs and adverbs beginning with *re-*, e.g., *repeatedly, return, restore, retell, replace, renew,* (If he
*re*turns before I leave, I want to talk to him.)———→
(He has been here before.)

(l)   **Qualifiers.** *Only, even, except, just*
(*Only* Amy saw the bank robbers.)———→(Amy
saw the bank robbers.)

(m)   **Change-of-Place Verbs.** *Come, go, leave, arrive, depart,
enter*
(If Sam has *left* home, he is lost.)———→(Sam has
been at home.)

(n)   **Change-of-Time Verbs and Adverbs.** *Begin, end, stop,
start, continue, proceed, already, yet, still, anymore*
(My bet is that Harry will *continue* to smile.)———→
(Harry has been smiling.)

(o)   **Change-of-State Verbs.** *Change, transform, turn into,
become*
(If Mae *turns into* a hippie, I'll be surprised.)———→
(Mae is not now a hippie.)

(p)   **Factive Verbs and Adjectives.** *Odd, aware, know,
realize, regret*
(It is *odd* that she called Maxine at midnight.)
———→(She called Maxine at midnight.)

(q) **Commentary Adjectives and Adverbs.** *Lucky, fortunately, far out, out of sight, groovy, bitchin, . . . innocently, happily, necessarily*

    (It's *far out* that you understand your dog's feelings.)———▶(You understand your dog's feelings.)

(r) **Counterfactual Conditional Clauses.**

    Verbs having subjunctive tense. (*If you had listened to me and your father,* you wouldn't be in the wonderful position you're in now.)———▶(You didn't listen to me and your father.)

(s) **Contrary-to-Expectation** *Should.*

    (*If you should [happen to]* decide you want to talk to me, I'll be hanging out in the city dump.)———▶(I don't expect you want to talk to me.)

(t) **Selectional Restrictions.**

    (If my professor gets *pregnant*, I'll be disappointed.)———▶(My professor is a woman.)

(u) **Questions.**

    (Who ate the tapes?)———▶(Someone ate the tapes.) (I want to know who ate the tapes.)———▶ (Someone ate the tapes.)

(v) **Negative Questions.**

    (Did*n't* you want to talk to me?)———▶(I thought that you wanted to talk to me.)

(w) **Rhetorical Questions.**

    (Who cares whether you show up or not?)———▶ (Nobody cares whether you show up or not.)

(x) **Spurious** *Not.*

    (I wonder if you're *not* being a little unfair.)———▶ (I think that you're being unfair.)

Glossary

Ambiguity: The name of the experience that people have with sentences that mean more than one thing, e.g., *Murdering peasants can be dangerous.* This sentence is understood by native speakers of English in two ways: (1) where the peasants mentioned are doing the murdering, and (2) where the peasants mentioned are being murdered. In the transformational model of language, a Surface Structure is said to be ambiguous if it can be derived from more than one Deep Structure.

Analogical: An adjective which describes any process which is continuous in nature. Two of the best known forms of analogical communication are body expression and voice tone.

Completeness: A logical semantic property of the full linguistic representation, the Deep Structure. Surface Structures are complete if they represent every portion of the Deep Structure.

Deep Structure: The full linguistic representation from which the Surface Structures of the language are derived.

Deletion: One of the three universals of human modeling; the process by which selected portions of the world are excluded from the representation created by the person modeling. Within language systems, deletion is a transformational process in which portions of the Deep Structure are removed and, therefore, do not appear in the Surface Structure representation.

Digital: An adjective which describes any process which is discrete in nature. The best known digital communication system is language.

Distortion: One of the three universals of human modeling; the process by which the relationships which hold among the parts of the model are represented differently from the relationships which they are supposed to represent. One of the most common examples of distortion in modeling is the representation of a process by an event. Within language systems, this is called *nominalization.*

Enrichment: The process of increasing the number of distinctions in a model. In therapy, the process by which a person comes to have more choices in his behavior.

Explicit: Presented in a step-by-step manner; not relying on interpretation.

Extentional: Definition by a listing of each specific member of the category being defined.

Formal: Used in two senses in this book: (1) explicit; (2) independent of content.

Generalization: One of the three universals of human modeling; the process by which a specific experience comes to represent the entire category of which it is a member.

Impoverishment: The process of limiting the number of distinctions in a model. In therapy, the process by which a person comes to have a small number of choices or no choice in his behavior.

Intensional: Definitional by a characteristic(s) of the members of the category being defined rather than by listing the specific members.

Intuition: Consistent judgments made by people (typically, without an explanation of how these judgments are made). Within language systems, the ability of native speakers of a language to make consistent judgments about the sentences of their language; for example, their ability to decide which sequences of words in their language are well-formed sentences. A classic example of human rule-governed behavior.

Meta-model: A representation of a representation of something. For example, language is a representation of the world of experience; transformational grammar is a representation of language and, therefore, a Meta-model.

Model/Modeling: A representation of something/the process of representing something; a map, for example. A process which involves the three processes of Generalization, Distortion, and Deletion.

Nominalization: The linguistic representation of a process by an event.

Presupposition: A basic underlying assumption which is necessary for a representation to make sense. Within language systems, a sentence which must be true for some other sentence to make sense.

Reference Structure: The sum total of experiences in a person's life history. Also, the fullest representation from which other representations within some system are derived; for example, the Deep Structure serves as the Reference Structure for Surface Structure.

Representation: An image of something which is different from the thing itself; a map, a model.

Rule-Governed Behavior: Behavior which is systematic and can be represented explicitly by a set of rules. In the case of human rule-governed behavior, no awareness of the rules is necessary.

Semantics: The study of meaning.

Synonymy: The name of the experience which people have with sentences of distinct form which have the same meaning; e.g., *The cat chased the rat* and *The rat was chased by the cat.* In the transformational model of language, two or more sentences are said to be synonymous if they are derived from the same Deep Structure.

Syntax: The study of the order and patterning of elements of a system. Within language, the study of the order and patterning of words and phrases.

Surface Structure: The sentences, derived from Deep Structure, which native speakers of the language speak and write.

Well-Formed: Meeting some set of conditions about form; e.g., well-formed in English, well-formed in therapy.

Bibliography

In this bibliography, our purpose is to provide references which will allow you to pursue any interests of which you have become aware in reading our book. We have divided the references into three sections:

Section I.
Transformational Grammar
Section II.
Therapy
Section III.
Modeling/Formal Systems/Epistemology

In each of these sections, we identify a small number of works which we have found particularly useful in developing our own models. The references given are not exhaustive, nor are they the only places where the ideas they contain can be found. We hope you enjoy your reading. If you know of other reference works which you have found particularly clear and useful in your experience in these areas, we would each appreciate hearing from you about them. Finally, if you wish to pursue some idea or line of thought or experience set off by our book and the bibliography is inadequate for your purposes, write to us and we will each try to suggest references for you.

META-MODELS
c/o Science and Behavior Books, Inc.
P.O. Box 11457
Palo Alto, CA 94306

I. **Transformational Grammar**
   A. *Basic References*
   Bach, E. *Syntactic Theory.* New York: Holt, Rinehart and Winston, Inc., 1974. A carefully presented overview of syntax as done by transformationalists.

   Chomsky, N. *Syntactic Structures.* The Hague: Mouton, 1957. The book which established the transformational model in linguistics; the style Chomsky uses is difficult for many readers. The portions of the book most connected with the Meta-model are the Preface; Chapters 2, 3, 5, 6, 8; and the Summary.

   Chomsky, N. *Aspects of the Theory of Syntax.* Cambridge, Mass.: MIT Press, 1965. This is one of the most accessible descriptions of the linguistic model from which we have borrowed heavily. Again, some readers find the author's style difficult. We especially recommend Chapters 1 and 2.

   Chomsky, N. *Language and Mind.* New York: Harcourt Brace Jovanovich, Inc., 1968. Four lectures which Chomsky gave as a visiting professor at Berkeley; less technical than his other two works we list.

   Grinder, J., and Elgin, S. *A Guide to Transformational Grammar.* New York: Holt, Rinehart and Winston, 1973. A very comprehensive overview of the entire field of transformational grammar; includes summaries of, and commentaries on, Chomsky's *Syntactic Structures* and *Aspects.* See especially Chapters 1, 2, 4, 5, 6, 7, 8, 10, and 13.

   Jacobs, R., and Rosenbaum, P. *English Transformational Grammar.* Waltham, Mass.: Ginn/Blaisdell, 1968. A very readable work as an introduction to the field; not particularly comprehensive.

   Langacker, R. *Language and Its Structure.* New York: Harcourt Brace Jovanovich, Inc., 1967. A readable introduction which treats language both by the transformational model and more generally.

   Lyons, J. *Introduction to Theoretical Linguistics.* Cambridge, England: Cambridge University Press. A scholarly work which presents an overview of language in general; includes a section on the transformational model.

   B. *Other Useful Transformational Work*
   Bever, T. G. "The Cognitive Basis of Linguistic Structure."

In J. Hayes (ed.), *Cognition and the Developments of Language*. New York: John Wiley and Sons, 1970. An excellent account of how language as a representational system might be connected to general modeling abilities of human beings — especially the way that children develop these abilities.

Fillmore, C. "The Case for Case." In E. Bach and R. Harms (eds.), *Universals in Linguistic Theory*. New York: Holt, Rinehart and Winston, 1968. A readable account of a somewhat different version of the transformational model — useful suggestions about what a complete representation of reference structure might be.

Greene, G. "How to Get People to Do Things With Words." In *Papers from the 8th Regional Meeting of the Chicago Linguistic Society*. Chicago, Ill.: University of Chicago, 1970. An excellent example of the Generative Semantics approach which we feel will contribute much to an enlarged Meta-model for therapy.

Grinder, J. *On Deletion Phenomena in English*. The Hague: Mouton, 1974. Very technical; useful for discussion of different types of deletion. See Chapters 1, 2, and 3.

Gruber, J. "Studies in Lexical Relations." Unpublished doctoral dissertation, MIT, 1965. Excellent suggestion for a complete representation of reference structures.

Horn, L. "A Presuppositional Analysis of *Only* and *Even*." In *Papers from the 5th Regional Meeting of the Chicago Linguistic Society*. Chicago, Ill.: University of Chicago, 1969. Another fine example of the Generative Semantics type of research which we feel will contribute to an enlarged Meta-model for therapy.

Kartunnen, L. "Remarks on Presuppositions." At the Texas Conference on Performances, Conversational Implicature and Presuppositions, mimeograph, March 1973. Kartunnen has a series of incisive papers on presuppositional phenomena in English. We suggest you write to him directly at the University of Texas for copies.

Katz, J. *Semantic Theory*. New York: Harper and Row, 1972. A most up-to-date account of the kind of semantic theory most compatible with non-Generative Semantics transformational grammar.

Lakoff, G. *Linguistics and Natural Logic*. Ann Arbor, Mich.: University of Michigan, 1970. A valuable compendium of some of the more recent work in Generative Semantics by its most prolific spokesperson. G. Lakoff is presently at the University of California, Berkeley.

McCawley, J. "Lexical Insertion in a Transformational Grammar." In *Papers from the 4th Regional Meeting of the Chicago Linguistic Society.* Chicago, Ill.: University of Chicago, 1968. One of the initial articles establishing Generative Semantics; good suggestions about the representation of reference structures.

Postal, P. "On the Derivation of Pseudo-Adjectives." Paper delivered to the 44th Annual Meeting of the LSA, 1969.

Postal, P. "On the Surface Verb *Remind.*" In *Linguistic Inquiry, 1;* 1:37-120. Postal's work is highly theoretical; the first reference has excellent examples of the patterns of derivation as Deep Structure Predicates are mapped into Surface Structure Adjectives. The second reference is very useful in making suggestions about the representation of reference structures.

Ross, J. R. "On Declarative Sentences." In R. Jacobs and P. Rosenbaum, *Readings in English Transformational Grammar.* Waltham, Mass.: Ginn/Blaisdell, 1970. This is the linguistic basis for the section in Chapter 4 called *The Last Performative* and an excellent example of linguistic analysis.

Sapir, E. *The Selected Writing of Edward Sapir.* D. Mandelbaum (ed.). University of California Press, Berkeley, 1963. One of the classical linguists who had a fine sensitivity for modeling.

Searle, J. *Speech Acts.* Cambridge, England: Cambridge University Press, 1969. A modern work in pragmatics with the transformational model as a basis. Readable.

Whorf, B. "Grammatical Categories." In J. E. Carroll (ed.), *Language, Thought and Reality.* New York: John Wiley and Sons, 1956. Another classical linguist who addressed the issue of the way language shapes perception.

II. Therapy

Jackson, D. D. *Communication, Family and Marriage.* Palo Alto: Science and Behavior Books, 1968. An excellent anthology containing the papers of the MRI/Bateson research group.

Jackson, D. D. *Therapy, Communication and Change.* Palo

Alto: Science and Behavior Books, 1968. An excellent anthology containing the papers of the MRI/Bateson research group.

Haley, J. *Advanced Techniques of Hypnosis and Therapy: Selected Papers of Milton H. Erickson, M.D.* New York: Grune and Stratton, 1967. An incredible collection of papers describing the powerful techniques of Milton Erickson.

Haley, J. *Uncommon Therapy.* New York: Grune and Stratton, 1968. A valuable statement of Erickson's powerful work with an interesting commentary by Jay Haley.

Perls, F. *The Gestalt Approach: Eyewitness to Therapy.* Palo Alto: Science and Behavior Books, 1973. A clear presentation of Gestalt therapy theoretical foundations.

Polster, I. and M. *Gestalt Therapy Integrated.* New York: Bruner/Mazel, 1973. A useful presentation of some of the techniques of Gestalt therapy.

Satir, V. *Conjoint Family Therapy.* Palo Alto: Science and Behavior Books, 1964. A basic and most useful text on family therapy.

Satir, V. *Peoplemaking.* Palo Alto: Science and Behavior Books, 1972. An excellent and highly readable introduction to communications and therapy.

Watzlawick, P.; Beavin, J.; and Jackson, D. *Pragmatics of Human Communications.* New York: W. Norton, 1967. A highly readable presentation of Bateson's ideas (e.g., meta-communication).

Watzlawick, P.; Weakland, J.; and Fisch, R. *Change.* New York: W. Norton, 1974. An interesting attempt to integrate mathematical models with patterns of human change.

III. Modeling/Formal Systems/Epistemology

Ashby, W. R. *An Introduction to Cybernetics.* Chapman and Hall, Ltd., and University Paperbacks, 1956. An excellent introduction to modelings and representational systems; requires some mathematical background; worth working through carefully.

Bateson, G. *Steps to an Ecology of Mind.* New York: Ballantine Books, 1972. We recommend this book highly; it is a collection of Bateson's work. Very entertaining; simultaneously irrelevant and profound.

Boyd, D. *Introduction to Systems Analysis,* (in press) 1975. A highly readable, clear presentation of modeling; emphasizes process.

Carnap, R. *The Logical Syntax of Language.* Totowa, New Jersey: Littlefield, Adams and Company, 1959. A formal, sophisticated approach to linguistic analysis. A highly technical piece of work; difficult to read.

Copi, I. *Introduction to Logic.* New York: Macmillan, 1961. An excellent introductory text to logical systems.

Herzberger, H. "The Logical Consistency of Language." *Harvard Educational Review, 35*:469-480; 1965. An example of a clear philosophical analysis of one of the formal properties of the human representational system of language.

Hume, D. *Enquiry Concerning Human Understanding.* Oxford, England: Oxford University Press. A classical essay on epistemology, the process of human modeling.

Korzybski, A. *Science and Sanity.* Lakeville, Connecticut: The International Non-Aristotelian Library Publishing Company, 4th Edition, 1933. The basic reference work for general semantics. Korzybski understood and discussed clearly the map/territory, intentional/extensional distinctions, . . . in human modeling. Read the Prefaces, Part I, and Part II.

Miller, G. A.; Galanter, E.; and Pribram, K. *Plans and the Structure of Behavior.* New York: Holt, Rinehart and Winston, Inc., 1960. One of the clearest presentations of a theoretical basis for human behavior; suggestions for a representational system for reference structures; easy and enjoyable reading.

Newell, A.; and Simon, H. A. *Human Problem Solving.* Englewood Cliffs, New Jersey: Prentice-Hall, 1971. An exciting excursion into the neurological basis for human modeling. A clear presentation.

Russell, B. *Introduction to Mathematical Philosophy.* London, England: George Allen and Unwin, Ltd., 2nd Edition, 1921. A readable, clear presentation of some of the more important concepts of modern logic, including theory of logical types.

Schank, R.; and Colby, K. *Computer Models of Thought and Language.* San Francisco: W. H. Freeman and Company, 1973. A good, representative collection of modeling as done in computer simulations.

Tarski, A. *Introduction to Logic.* New York: Oxford University Press, 1941. An excellent introduction to logical systems, a very readable style, no background required.

Vaihinger, H. *The Philosophy of "As If."* London, England: Routledge, Kegan and Paul, Ltd., 1924. An excellent source for discussions of human modeling. F. Perls claimed Vaihinger supplied the philosophical foundations for his Gestalt therapy.

Watzlawick, P.; Beavin, J.; and Jackson, D. *Pragmatics of Human Communication.* New York: W. W. Norton and Company, 1967. A very readable, clear presentation of some of the basic ideas of communication with connections to systems analysis.